W9-CMV-278

Enhance
your
life
experience

Dr. Joseph B. Strauss

© 1996
F.A.C.E.
P.O. Box 1052
Levittown, PA 19058
Faucet and Bucket illustration by Richard Dempsey, Jr.

Dedicated to all those
who are interested in a healthier,
more productive life
and are willing to do
what is necessary to achieve it.

Table of Contents

1

TAKE CONTROL!

There is an old saying,
"Everyone wants to go to heaven but nobody wants to die to do it." We feel the same way about our health. Everybody wants to be healthy but no one wants to do the necessary things to get there. The fact is, health comes from within you. You cannot buy it at the local pharmacy. A wise man once said, "if health came in a bottle, there would be a shortage of bottles." It cannot be given to you by someone. It is not contagious. You may receive a genetic predisposition toward health from your parents, but that is only a tendency. That predisposition must be turned into a healthy life by you, by the decisions you make and the action you take. Those decisions and actions are literally a matter of life and death.

It's Your Life

Without doubt, the single most important concept to understand and accept so that you may attain maximum health and get the most out of life is that YOU are responsible for your health. You may receive information, advice, care or treatment from others, including health care professionals, but YOU are ultimately responsible for your health. That is really the way it should be. No one is as concerned about you as YOU are. Or should I say, as concerned about you as you should be. No one is able to understand what is going on in your body as well as YOU are, providing you learn to become aware. No one understands your body's needs as well as YOU do. No one is going to suffer the consequences of doing the wrong thing or reap the benefits of doing the right thing more than YOU. If you add ten years to your life or take ten years from your life, it's YOUR life!

A New Idea

The idea of taking control and responsibility for one's own health is a relatively recent concept. Throughout history the responsibility for peoples' health was assumed by the most learned and powerful person in the society. Witch doctors, medicine men and shamans (priests who use magic) were charged with matters of health and disease, and they became the most important persons in the community or village. Their life and death position added to their authority and perpetuated the cycle. Even as late as the middle part of the 20th century in the United States, a medical doctor was, to a great degree, the authority on matters of health and even child-rearing. Most American mothers used Benjamin Spock, M.D. as their authority in the 40's and 50's. In the 60's that changed slightly. The 60's generation of young people began to question and reject authority. A government that wanted to send them off to a questionable war was defied, parental values were rejected. The idea that the university student had no say in the education process was set aside and, to a degree, the role of the physician as the sole authority in matters of health was challenged.

Taking Back Control

During this same period many of the health care alternatives popular today began to gain acceptance. Today it is estimated that perhaps half the country's population will visit so-called "alternative health care providers" in the course of a year, despite the fact that most of these practices are still frowned upon by the traditional medical establishment. In a limited way these people are taking control of their health. They are telling the medical community that despite its warnings, criticisms and protests against the use of alternative health care systems, as well as the glorification of orthodox medicine by the media, they are choosing to do their own thing. They are choosing approaches that appeal to them perhaps because they are easier to understand, or they do not involve the use of drugs, or they just make sense. They may be choosing alternatives because they are dissatisfied with the medical approach for one reason or another. Whatever the case, it is clear that a substantial segment of the population is taking back control of their health from the medical establishment.

● ● ● ● ● ● ● ● ● ● ● ● ●

But... Giving It Away Again

Unfortunately, too many of these people are subsequently turning control of their health over to one of these alternative health care practitioners. For some, this may be an improvement. These are the people that are receiving unnecessary or poor medical care and would be better off with anything else. For others, this may be detrimental. These are the people who will reject life-saving medical procedures, because they are receiving a non-medical procedure that they believe in, but which will not help them. But for both these groups and everyone else, giving control of YOUR health to anyone (medical or alternative) is not in the best interest of YOUR life and well-being.

Professional knowledge and experience should be considered in light of your needs, desires, knowledge and perspective. In the end, you must decide that control of YOUR health and the responsibility for YOUR health and well-being rests squarely on YOUR shoulders. Without that decision and the commitment which must accompany it, you will never begin to experience maximum health. However, once making that conscious decision, you are ready to learn how to enhance your life experience!

This book is about giving you that perspective and hopefully setting you in a direction to gain the necessary knowledge to live a healthier life.

Are you in control of your health? The quiz on the following page will help you determine if you are. Answer it honestly. No one is looking over your shoulder.

•   •   •   •   •   •   •   •   •   •   •   •   •

Are You In Control?

☐ ☐ 1. Do you ever ask about the side-effects of pre-
N Y   scription medication?

☐ ☐ 2. Do you get second and even third opinions on a
N Y   physical problem?

☐ ☐ 3. Do you ever question the doctor about alternatives
N Y   to his recommendations or prescriptions?

☐ ☐ 4. Do you ever ask a health care provider about the
N Y   possible ramifications of a procedure?

☐ ☐ 5. Have you read a book, magazine, or newspaper
N Y   articles on health in the last two months?

☐ ☐ 6. If you were to choose the three most important
N Y   things in life, would your health be one of them?

☐ ☐ 7. Do you find yourself actually listening to drug
N Y   commercials on television?

☐ ☐ 8. Do you assume that a procedure, because it is
N Y   drugless, is better than a drug?

☐ ☐ 9. Do you think that health is mostly a matter of luck
N Y   and there is very little you can do about it one way
  or another?

☐ ☐ 10. Do you choose a health care provider based solely
N Y   upon any of the following: the provider's per-
  sonality, education, degree, authority, a friend or
  relative's recommendation, convenience.

If you answered "no" to any of the first six and "yes" to any of the last four questions, there is a good chance that you are not in control. If you want to assume that control, you can and will enhance your life experience. Before you can assume control, you must be convinced that you are capable enough. The next chapter will show you that you and your body are best qualified to make decisions and take control.

• • • • • • • • • • • • •

YOUR
AMAZING BODY

Flames engulfed a New York City
apartment building. At a fifth floor window stood a small
four-year-old girl. The firefighters could not get to her but
they held a safety net on the street below and encouraged her
to jump. Despite the fact that the flames were getting closer
and closer to her, the child was too frightened to leap from the
window to the waiting net fifty feet beneath her. The fireman
continued their pleas to no avail, and just when it appeared
that the child's life would be lost, her father appeared on the
scene. He stood next to the net and called his daughter by
name. He gently but firmly assured her that she would be fine,
and that she should jump. With those words the child leapt to
safety. What was the difference between the firemen's pleas
and the father's? The child knew her father and trusted him.
The more we know about the human body, the more we can

appreciate and trust the principle of life which has been called by various names, such as "the wisdom of the body" and the "innate intelligence of the body." The more we understand and appreciate this principle, the greater our ability to truly understand and experience health.

Most people do not have confidence in the body's ability to run and heal itself. At the first sign or symptom of what appears to them as sickness or disease, they run off to a doctor for advice or treatment. If we can understand a little about how wonderful the body is and what it is capable of doing, we will put more confidence in its ability to stay healthy and even to restore health and heal itself when it does appear to be sick or injured.

True Health Care

There are dozens of professions that claim to be part of the health field. The basis for a true health care profession is the recognition of the presence of a wisdom, a principle of organization, which runs the body better than any educated mind. We will refer to it as the "innate intelligence of the body." It is resident within every living organism. In the human being, it is present from the moment of conception until the moment of death. The innate intelligence is the principle that is responsible for the organization of living matter. It separates that which is living from that which is not. Every living thing demonstrates this same principle. It is the same in a one-celled amoebae as it is in a human being. It is the same in a one-day-old baby as it is in a ninety-nine-year-old man. It is no greater or less in the genius than in the severely retarded. It does not increase or decrease, no matter what we do or where we go to college. We are born with all the innate intelligence we will ever need. It may, perhaps, be the only factor that makes "all men created equal." It causes all the components of a cell to act in an organized manner, creating the smallest unit of life. It organizes cells together to form a tissue. It organizes very different tissues to work together in an organized manner - we even call that structure an "organ." Lastly, this principle of organization, this innate intelligence, organizes all the systems together to form a living human being. A corpse may have all the same organs and parts but it is lacking an innate intelligence.

Applying the Principle

The recognition of this principle of life is not unique to any specific healing art, although it may be known by many different descriptive terms. Boyd's Pathology refers to it as "the wisdom of the body." It has often been referred to as "Mother Nature" and by other terms. What is unique about true health care professions is not the mere recognition of this principle but the practical application of it on a day-to-day basis in each and every aspect of health. It is not a theoretical-philosophical concept to be placed on a shelf and then forgotten but a practical day-to-day principle to be applied to one's health.

There is a principle in logic called "afortiori," a Latin term meaning "with greater force" or "all the more." Basically the principle is that someone or something capable of accomplishing the greater is all the more capable of accomplishing something less. For example, if I can throw a baseball 200 feet, it follows afortiori that I can throw a

● ● ● ● ● ● ● ● ● ● ● ● ●

baseball 50 feet. If I can lift a 100 lb. barbell, it follows afortiori that I can lift a 10 lb. bag of potatoes.

The principle or law of innate intelligence goes into effect the moment a sperm and egg unite. Without any thought on our part, without any encouragement from us and even without our knowledge, this principle causes the cells to begin to divide and form a human being. That formation takes place to a great extent before the mother-to-be is even aware that she is pregnant. As this one cell begins to divide, something unique happens. Logic would say that all the reproduced cells would be like the original. But as time goes on the cells begin to form different types of tissues. Some become what will eventually be heart tissue, some kidney tissues, some skin, some bones. How do these cells know to do that? The communication system, the nervous system is not even formed yet. But even at the moment of conception, the union of those two cells contains all the information, the programming to determine eye and hair color, facial characteristics and everything else that makes a person unique. Contained within is all the information

> All the DNA information necessary to design every human being could be combined in a space the size of a dime!

to build two eyes, two ears, a nose, a mouth, ten little fingers and toes and to put them all in the right place! We may not know whether it will be a boy or a girl or whose side of the family it will resemble but we know where all the parts will be located! It is all contained within the DNA of those two cells. We are amazed at the capabilities of computers. One CD can

•   •   •   •   •   •   •   •   •   •   •   •

contain all the information in an entire set of encyclopedias. New technology in the computer field will soon be doing even better. Yet, all the information in the DNA necessary to design human beings, the "blueprints" of every member of the human race on the face of the earth at this very moment, could be combined and contained in the space the size of a dime!

That blueprint is followed for each person as the innate intelligence "builds" a human body in nine months. It first forms what will be the brain and nervous system and then adds all the parts.

If the innate intelligence of the body is capable of building a body in nine months without any outside help from a medical doctor, or anyone else, then it follows afortiori that the innate intelligence of the body is capable of running and repairing the body for the next 80 to 120 years. Building the human body is the tough job, repairing it is a snap in comparison. We marvel at newborns as beautiful creations, and yet, we believe that their bodies cannot work properly for a lifetime without outside help. We constantly turn to educated minds to run them for us. The fact is that all the educated minds in the world could not build one single, living cell. Yet, your body does it billions of times a day!

> The innate intelligence that creates the body in nine months can run it for the entire lifetime

There is another important principle that is part of the foundation for this unique approach to health care. It too is related to the innate intelligence of the body. It is the fact that every member of the human race is a unique individual. The

•　•　•　•　•　•　•　•　•　•　•　•　•

innate intelligence may be the same in all living things but the matter (the material) that it is working through is different. Even members of the same species are different. You only need to look at the various people on a crowded bus to realize we are all unique. If people are physically unique, then their norms and needs are unique to them, a concept we will discuss in detail in Chapter 5. Understanding the uniqueness of each individual is important. Every student of anatomy has studied the "Circle of Willis" which is the main blood supply to the brain. The blood vessels making up this structure take up almost two pages of Gray's Anatomy in description. It takes the average student hours to memorize it. However, at the bottom of the page is a small footnote saying that the diagram is only correct for 40% of the population. That means over half the bodies examined in preparing the text had some variation in anatomical structure. We are as different on the inside as we are on the outside. We all may have two eyes, a nose and a mouth but we are different in many other ways. There are eight basic fingerprint patterns in the human body yet no two are alike. They have also established voiceprints and found that no two are identical and it does not matter whether you are shouting, whispering or talking with marbles in your mouth, your voiceprint is unique to you! Our internal structure is as different as our external structure. It is widely understood in science that structure determines how something functions, so it follows that the function of each person is unique for that individual. Let's take a look at some of the amazing ways your body is designed.

•   •   •   •   •   •   •   •   •   •   •   •

The Defense System

In understanding and appreciating the human body one only has to look at its defense system. The white blood cells (leukocytes) are the fighting troops of the body. They live for only a few days. The body is constantly producing new ones to replace those that die. On any given day there are 30-40 billion white blood cells on duty to fight infections and foreign organisms. The moment you cut your finger, millions of these blood cells are moved into the area to fight a potential infection. It has only recently been discovered that there are greater numbers of these white blood cells in the tonsils, lungs, the lymph nodes and the appendix making these important areas of first-line defense. Since these findings, medical science has ceased, if only gradually, the unnecessary removal of the appendix and the tonsils. It is important to note that not being aware of their function did not make those organs any less important.

The Life Blood

The blood of the human body is one of nature's most amazing fluids. A drop of it, just 1/25th of an inch, contains five million red blood cells (erythrocytes), 7,000 white blood cells and thousands of platelets. A red blood cell lives about 120 days and during that time it makes 300,000 trips through your blood stream, almost two times every minute! 10,000 wear out every second. If one could take all the red blood cells in the body and place them one on top of another like a stack of coins, the pile would stretch half way to the moon! Yet, every one of them dies in 4 months and is replaced by new healthy ones at a rate of 3 million every second (providing the body is healthy).

The Irreplaceable Heart

Not too long ago the medical profession was excited about the idea of artificial hearts. Today it is very common to hear of a heart transplant on the news. Considering the shortage of donors, why is it that the use of artificial hearts is not a more common procedure? Perhaps part of the reason is the inability of biomedical engineers to develop a mechanical heart that can replace the human heart. Science, with all its technology that "can put a man on the moon," has practically given up on the idea of artificial hearts. They simply cannot build one to replace the original. The human heart weighs less than a pound yet it beats 40 million times a year. The arteries and veins, "the plumbing system" in your body, if stretched out, would cover a distance of about 12,000 miles. Imagine having a pump that would pump fluid a distance of 12,000 miles! The heart pumps 2.5 gallons per minute or 1,314,000 gallons a year through those arteries and veins. Man has not come close to inventing a pump that can perform like the human heart.

The Lungs

The lungs are a beautiful example of how design benefits function. The lungs use about 90 gallons of pure oxygen every day. There are little sacs called "alveoli" which are finger-like projections lining the walls of the lungs. Each of your lungs is not much longer than an outstretched hand, yet the inside surface of them with these projections is approximately 40-60 square miles! Imagine having 40-60 square miles of surface area in your chest! You breathe approximately 9 million times a year, pumping air at the rate of two gallons a minute when at rest and 26 gallons per minute when exercising.

So Much Activity!

These are only a very few examples of all the functions your body is performing at this very moment. The coordination of all this activity demonstrates the law of life, the innate intelligence. Coordinated activity is an indication of intelligence. Whenever we see organization or coordinated activity, we know there is some intelligence behind it. Nothing organizes itself. The human body is the most organized thing in the world. Billions upon billions of cells work together in a coordinated manner, each doing its job to benefit the whole. There are more than 600 muscles in your body. To press a barbell over your head takes the action of 200 of them, 31 in your face alone.

Within the healthy body, every moment, there are thousands of chemicals being produced in just the right quantity and quality to carry on every function necessary to life and health. Just think for a moment what happens when you put food into your mouth. Chemicals called "enzymes" are produced to begin the digestion process while the food is still in the mouth. Some say even before you eat, olfactory (smell) sensors triggered by the aroma of food cooking begin the chemical production necessary for optimal digestion of that food. Some also argue that increased gastrointestinal symptoms in today's society may be due to a lack of this

•   •   •   •   •   •   •   •   •   •   •   •   •

trigger mechanism due to the use of previously prepared (fast or frozen) foods. When you swallow, the epiglottis closes, (the small trap door in your throat that prevents food from going into your lungs.) You don't think about it or will it. It just happens innately. The food then passes down the esophagus into the stomach. Maybe you think, "No big deal. It's gravity, like a drain pipe." But actually, it is not gravity. It is the action of the muscles lining the wall of the esophagus. You could swallow food while hanging upside-down and it would still pass into your stomach! Once in the stomach, strong acids are produced to break down the food. This acid is so strong that a drop of it on your skin would leave a painful blister. Your body provides 2 1\2 quarts of this acid every day, over 60 thousand quarts of it to digest 40 tons of food over a 70 year period and yet it does not eat a hole in the lining of your stomach! The walls of the stomach constantly produce a mucous-like substance that protects them from damage. Once the food passes through the stomach, the process of "assimilation" takes place. The food is made into flesh and blood. All of this is occurring while we are going about our daily activities, totally oblivious to what is happening. It's just as well because any thought on our part would not help the process one bit. In the small intestine, the body begins to extract what it needs from the food. It demonstrates selectivity, absorbing the necessary substances like vitamins, minerals, and sugars to be used by the body. It only takes what is necessary, passing along what it cannot use. In the large intestine, fluid is absorbed for use in the body and you are informed by your body to get rid of everything that is not usable. We can be grateful that this process is innate. If we had to think about everything occurring from the time we swallowed our food, we would not have any time during the course of the day to do anything else!

Most of us are familiar with Pavlov's experiment in which he fed dogs at the sound of a bell until they began to salivate by the ringing of the bell alone. But a little known experiment was done by the scientist which demonstrates the innate intelligence in the digestive process. He took a number of dogs and surgically altered them so that the food that they swallowed would not pass into their stomach but out a tube instead. He then had another tube drain off the gastric juices produced in the stomach. In the experiment, he gave four different foods to the dogs and collected the juices from the stomach. He then sent the four jars out to a laboratory to be analyzed. Each jar contained the exact combination of juices necessary to digest the specific foods even though the food had never passed into the dogs' stomachs! While in the mouth, the innate intelligence of the body sent the message to the stomach to produce gastric juices for digestion, and not just any gastric juice, but that of a quality precisely appropriate for the type of food in the dog's mouth. If you have ever seen a dog eat, you know that the food does not stay in its mouth for a very long period of time. Yet it is long enough for the body to know the character of the food and send a message to the stomach to begin the digestive process specifically for that food!

These facts about the human body are amazing and incredible and only a small sample of the wondrous complex workings of our bodies. The purpose in presenting them is to develop in you an appreciation for the wisdom that runs your body. While we marvel at the instrument, the creation, we must give the credit to the Builder and Creator. We admire a beautiful painting but the paint and the canvas are not the objects of our admiration and appreciation, it is the artist and his or her talent that deserves the credit. After a beautiful symphonic concert, we do not applaud the violins, french horns and tympany. We acknowledge the musicians. An appreciation and respect for the innate intelligence of the body is the essence of a viewpoint of life that focuses on health.

Once we have decided that we want control of our lives and health and we have an appreciation for the body's ability to be healthy, there is one remaining thing to do before we start. That is to begin to look at health differently.

3

LET'S LOOK AT HEALTH DIFFERENTLY

We desperately need to look at health in a different way and act in a manner consistent with our changing view. If we do not, the present system and its ramifications threaten us more than we realize. The government is wrestling with the real problem of providing health-care coverage for all Americans. They are doing it because the soaring costs of health care are threatening the average American. Yet in every country where government-managed health care has been tried, it has proven to be a miserable failure both in quality of care and in cost. The government feels it must do something even if that something is wrong, and it is. There has never been a situation where the government has been successful in running a program better than private industry. But private industry is incapable of solving the health-care problem as well. According to a recent statement by Ralph Nader, the number of Caesarean-section births has quadrupled in the last ten years. Obviously, the expense of childbirth goes up in these cases. Why is it happening? There are two likely reasons. The first is that women are not as healthy today, putting them at greater risk in trying to deliver naturally. The second reason is that if children are born with damage, the doctor and the hospital are likely to be sued. The technology to keep these poor children alive for years exists but it is costly, and the insurance company ends up with the bill. So doctors perform C-sections when there appears to be the slightest stress in the birth process. As long as the health of the mother-to-be does not improve, there will be stress. Our focus needs to be on keeping them healthy.

The incidence of "iatrogenic" diseases is becoming a real problem. These are diseases caused by doctors and their procedures. Estimates are as high as one out of every four hospital admissions being due to a medical procedure that left the patient worse off and in need of hospitalization. There is a reason. To become more and more successful in waging the battle against disease, more drastic measures are needed and they do increasingly more harm to the human organism. The success that medicine has had in treating diseases is due in part to the powerful drugs and highly technical procedures that are being used. But they have their harmful side effects and their dangers. The more success we have at combating diseases, the greater the number of casualties we can expect.

•   •   •   •   •   •   •   •   •   •   •   •

A Better Option

No matter how time consuming and expensive it is to develop and follow programs of health maintenance, it is far less expensive in time, money, energy and lives than is the treatment of disease. But with few exceptions the medical community continues treating, researching and focusing on disease. Little is done in orthodox medicine to ever consider an alternative to the treatment of disease. At best, they are looking toward alternative treatments of disease but not an alternative TO the treatment of disease. The following short story illustrates this point. As you read it, seriously consider the analogies, as well as the ramifications of our current "health care" system and its thinking.

Digging Up Holes -a short story

The front yard had mysteriously acquired large gaping holes sometime through the night. George Hunt surveyed the once beautiful lawn with the feeling that one has when they lose a dear friend or relative. It was not just the area between the house and street. This was George's child, his love, it occupied every moment of the confirmed bachelor's early evenings until the sun set, from April 1st until November 30th. He knew the neighbors would be gathering soon. Some would offer condolences. George could not bear the thought of them telling him they knew how he felt. They could not know. They had not spent the hours tenderly caring for their lawns the way he had. None except for Ben Warton. But even Ben's beautiful lawn could not hold a candle to George's. George knew Ben was jealous. There was almost a competitive spirit between them and not a friendly competition at that. Ben would surely gloat over George's misfortune.

The large white truck arrived late in the afternoon. It was very professional looking. Printed on the side in large, bold, black letters were the words:

DR. JOHN B. PITFALL
LAWN PHYSICIAN

•   •   •   •   •   •   •   •   •   •   •   •   •

A tall, thin, distinguished gentleman stepped out of the truck. He had on a crisp, white coat and a large mop of snowy white hair to match. His face was tanned and confident. A faint glimmer of hope welled up in George's heart. This man was the best Lawn Physician in the entire Eastern United States. George had felt honored when Dr. Pitfall had agreed to take on his case.

"Thank you for coming, Doctor." George tried to sound calm, despite the fact that his heart was beating madly.

"I don't usually take cases this far from my office, Mr. Hunt, but your case intrigues me. When did you first notice this problem?"

"Just this morning, doctor. The lawn was fine yesterday."

"Ever have a similar problem?"

"No, never."

"How about your lawn's general health?"

George took pride in his healthy lawn. But he realized this was not a time for bragging. He racked his brain for any indication of what could have caused this problem. After careful thought he responded, "Other than chinch bugs two years ago and some occasional brown spots in late July, the lawn has been fine."

The doctor stroked his smooth chin and scanned the homes up and down the street. "Any of your neighbors have this type of problem?"

"No, sir!"

"Okay, Mr. Hunt, we're going to be doing a few tests. Why don't you go in the house. My assistants will be along shortly and we'll be bringing some heavy equipment in. Out here you'll just be in the way."

George dutifully obeyed the doctor. Once in the house he drew open the drapes at the picture window, pulled over the easy chair, and sat down to watch. What he saw was impressive. The lawn physician and his assistants went to work with the skill of a finely-trained team. They took pictures of all the holes, every one of them, from every conceivable angle. George noticed the doctor talking to one of his assistants, a big burly fellow. The man nodded as if concurring with Dr. Pitfall's observation and then drove off in the truck. Thirty minutes later he returned with what appeared to be a large measuring device. He went to each hole, measuring the depth and the width and noting the slope of each one. A nurse followed him around making notations on a clipboard. George could not hear what they were saying through the thick window panes but the serious looks on their faces were anything but encouraging. The activities went on for the better part of two hours. George was impressed by their workman-like attitude but at the same time somewhat annoyed at their apparent detachment. Didn't they realize this was his one and only front yard?

●　　●　　●　　●　　●　　●　　●　　●　　●　　●　　●　　●

It was getting on toward dark. George had not left the picture window since the examination began. Finally Dr. Pitfall, aware of George observing them, motioned for him to come out.

"We would like to do a few more tests tomorrow Mr. Hunt, and I have a colleague I would like to call in on consultation. He'll be here tomorrow also. We should have some news for you the day after."

"What do you think it is, doctor?"

"I'd really not like to venture a guess until all the tests are done and the results are calculated. We have to go back to the office now and run a lot of these figures through our computers. We'll see you in the morning." With that, they all climbed into their trucks. Neither the trucks nor the doctors and nurses looked quite as white and crisp as they had earlier in the day. George was left standing among the holes in his yard as they drove off in the direction of the setting summer sun.

They returned the next day as promised and worked from early morning until almost sunset. Then left without a word. They returned the following day. There were more tests, more pictures. Each time there was one or more new faces. All had the same white coat, same tan, same serious expression. On the fourth day they did not return. Midway through the morning George received a phone call from Dr. Pitfall's office. The doctor would be coming to speak with George.

Shortly after noon he arrived.

"Sit down, Mr. Hunt."

George dreaded those words. Whenever a doctor on television tells someone to sit down, it's always bad news.

"George, I'm going to be honest with you. This is by far the worst case of holes in the lawn that I or any of my colleagues have ever seen. To be perfectly frank, it doesn't look good."

George had been sitting on the edge of his easy chair, the one he had spent the better part of the last four days in. He slumped back and spoke, his voice faltering, "what can be done, doctor?"

The doctor walked over to the window and gazed out upon the lawn as if to give it one further examination before pronouncing its fate. "The only hope is," he paused for what seemed an eternity to George, "major surgery. I'm afraid George, unless we dig up those holes, your lawn hasn't a chance."

George sat up straight. "You mean you're going to remove the holes?"

"That's right."

"But doctor, how can you remove a hole? I mean," George stammered trying to find the right words. His mind was spinning. "I mean, how can you dig up a hole?"

● ● ● ● ● ● ● ● ● ● ● ●

The doctor gave George a condescending smile. It irritated George. "Oh, we have a fine instrument. We can be in and out of here in one morning. It can remove every hole, take it right out. I have to admit it is a rather untried procedure, but frankly George, I see no other hope."

George rubbed his temples with his fingertips. "I just don't know."

"Look George, if you would like a second or third opinion I could give you the names..."

"No, doctor, I'm sure you're right. It's just, it doesn't seem... I just can't believe... it doesn't seem possible that digging up the holes is the answer." George got up and walked over to the picture window. He stared at his lawn remembering the lush green carpet that he had mown only a week ago. He turned sharply, looked the doctor in the eye and said, "when can you do the operation?"

"We will be here Monday morning."

George rarely ever opened the drapes of the front picture window. When leaving his house, and he only left to go to work or the store, he avoided looking at the front yard. It had been almost a month since the operation. Even before the big machinery began tearing into the soft, rich, dark earth George had this gnawing feeling that it wouldn't work. Dr. Pitfall had tried to cheer him up by saying they were able to reduce the number of holes to only a few large ones. The neighbors' condolence cards were appreciated. Except for Ben Warton's. Suggesting that George put a large hedge around his front yard was in poor taste. There was one card, from Mrs. Deery up the street. She had suggested that George try a Lawn Restorer. As the sight of the lawn became more painful, George gave more thought to her suggestion. Finally one morning he called Dr. Thomas Cause, Lawn Restorer. The doctor arrived in a small pickup. It was not white. He did not wear white and there were no assistants with him. He was, however, a friendly, soft spoken, kindly fellow. He seemed genuinely concerned over George's plight. George began to relate the lawn's history to Dr. Cause but the doctor stopped him.

"Mr. Hunt, I know you've been through a good deal with your problem and you obviously have had some experts looking at your lawn. I don't pretend to be able to do something they could not do." George face dropped. The doctor was smiling. "However, Mr. Hunt, I believe I have something I can do for your lawn that will benefit it."

"You mean you can cure holes in the lawn?"

"No, I didn't say that. As a matter of fact I cannot cure any problem. But what I can do is restore dirt and frankly, Mr. Hunt, whatever condition your lawn has or doesn't have, it would be better off with a full complement of dirt. You see, a Lawn Restorer is really a dirt replacer." He went on to explain a little more about his philosophy. It made sense to George. After they had talked awhile longer George walked over to his lawn and looked into one of the large holes.

"Don't you want to see the pictures or read the Lawn Physician's reports?"

"It's not really necessary to my procedure, Mr. Hunt. We are not really doing the same thing. He's removing holes, I'm replacing dirt."

George laughed aloud. "Well, I've gone the hole removal route and look what it's gotten me." He pointed to the gaping holes. "I guess I've got nothing to lose by trying... what did you call it?"

"Dirt replacement, Mr. Hunt."

"When can you begin?"

"I'll be here tomorrow with a truckload."

George thought for a minute, still not convinced he was doing the right thing. "But how will you know how much dirt my lawn needs without all the tests or at least looking at the Lawn Physician's report?"

"Good question, Mr. Hunt. I'll be in with a truckload tomorrow and begin to fill the holes. I'll just keep bringing truckloads until they are filled. It's really a very simple concept and procedure. When the holes are filled, my job is done."

The next day Dr. Cause returned, this time with a large truck full of dirt. He began to back it up toward the closest and largest hole. George raced out the front door.

"Hold it, doctor," he shouted over the roar of the truck engine. "Can I talk to you for a minute?"

The Lawn Restorer climbed out of the truck cab and the two of them walked a distance from the idling truck engine.

"What seems to be the problem, Mr. Hunt?"

George was somewhat embarrassed. "Can I be frank with you Dr. Cause?"

"But of course, please do. If there is anything you don't understand or want explained further, I would be very happy..."

"It's not that, it's just, well you see, I met this Lawn Therapist yesterday in the garden shop. He was buying a truckload of fertilizer and we got to talking. He called himself a Lawn Therapist Physician. He said I should have some tests done, that maybe my problem was a nutritional deficiency in the lawn. He also thought it might be six foot tall gophers. He said he would do those tests and sort of hinted that you should also."

"Let's sit down over here, Mr. Hunt. Remember I explained to you

• • • • • • • • • • • • •

that I am not a physician?"

"Yes."

"I do one thing only. I fill holes with dirt. Your lawn needs dirt. Whatever else it needs, it needs dirt. You must understand Mr. Hunt, I only am a 'dirt replacer.' You or someone else will have to take the responsibility for seeding, feeding, cutting, raking, watering and maintaining your lawn. I personally feel you are the person most qualified to do those things. However, sometimes you may need professional help. If you have six foot tall gophers, you may need a Lawn Exterminator. I am not trained or equipped to deal with gophers. Perhaps vandalism is your problem. I cannot sit here all night and protect your lawn. Do you see what I'm saying, Mr. Hunt? Your lawn has many needs. Under most circumstances you are the most qualified to meet those needs. From what I've seen of the other parts of your lawn, you do a fine job of taking care of it."

George felt his face flush with embarrassment. The Lawn Restorer continued, "But whatever your lawn needs and no matter who supplies those needs, one thing is for sure, it has no chance of being healthy and beautiful without a full complement of dirt. That is what I do."

"Dr. Cause, I'd like to have my dirt restored. Let's get to it!"

"Okay Mr. Hunt."

George stood back and watched the Lawn Restorer at work. His philosophy was different. His procedure was not orthodox lawn medicine. He didn't act like a lawn physician. But even as these thoughts raced through George's mind, he noticed that his holes were disappearing. With every truckload his lawn was returning. The "dirt restoration" was working.

Six weeks to the day after meeting the Lawn Restorer, George Hunt stood in front of his picture window. His lawn had returned to normal. Periodically Dr. Cause would come by and spread a little dirt here and there when needed. Other than that, there were no problems. George was a happy man. The neighbors were amazed. They marveled at the difference in George's lawn and told him so. It was once again the most beautiful lawn in the neighborhood. Prettier than Old Man Warton's front yard. It was definitely prettier than his back yard; which was full of piles of dirt that Warton claimed mysteriously appeared some time back.

The End

•   •   •   •   •   •   •   •   •   •   •   •

Of course, it seems rather absurd to view a hole as an "entity," something that has material existence and can be removed. Any rational person realizes that a hole is merely an absence of dirt. You can only create it by removing the dirt and you can only correct it by restoring dirt. But our health is no different. Disease is like the holes -it is the absence of health. Disease only occurs when health has been lost. Trying to remove disease is like trying to remove a hole. We need to begin to view *health* as the entity and disease as the non-entity, the absence of health.

Health and Disease

Science acknowledges both entities and non-entities. However, its attention is always directed toward the entity. Lets look at some examples.

Heat is an entity. It can be created by building a fire or burning some fossil fuel or gaseous substance. It can be measured in BTU's or calories. Cold, on the other hand, is merely the absence of heat. You cannot create cold. It merely is what exists when heat is withdrawn. It has certain characteristics -symptoms, if you will. When these symptoms are manifested, we do not have to listen to a weather report or even look at a thermometer. We say, "it's cold today!" It would be more correct to say "there's not much heat in the air today!" An air conditioner withdraws heat from a room leaving a room with a lack of heat. If you stand outside an air conditioner, you can feel the heat that has been withdrawn from the room.

Sound is an entity. We can create it by clapping our hands, speaking or turning on the radio. It is measured in

• • • • • • • • • • • •

decibels. Silence, on the other hand, is the absence of sound. It is a non-entity.

Light and darkness are probably the best examples. Light is the entity. We can create it by striking a match or flicking a switch. Darkness, on the other hand, is the non-entity. It is only manifested when the light or its source is removed. We measure light in watts or lumens. When the light is turned on, what happens to the darkness? It doesn't collect in a small pile in the corner or slip out under a crack in the door. It simply does not exist as a tangible entity. All the darkness in the world cannot extinguish the light from one candle. Darkness cannot overcome light.

Science deals with entities. But somehow when medicine began to investigate the issues of health and disease, they chose to make disease the entity and health the non-entity. Perhaps it is because the manifestations of disease are so much more noticeable than the manifestations of health. They are not the norm so they tend to stand out more. Regardless of why, the fact is that health is the normal state of an organism, so that when the organism manifests a lack of health, it catches our attention. It is very much like our analogy of light and darkness. We take light for granted. We think nothing of walking into a dark room, flipping a switch and have it suddenly be as bright as noon-day. If we had never seen it, perhaps we would be surprised, shocked or awed. But it becomes a normal act of everyday life. The same is true for a properly functioning healthy body. We don't go to bed at night and say, "Wow, my respiratory system really worked well today!" As we lay our head on our pillow at night very few of us reflect how our heart beat 103,680 times during the course of the day. We take health, like light, for granted. Most people when asked how they are, will say, "fine' or "okay" without really thinking about it. It's probably because we know that the person asking the question really does not want an organ-by-organ, system-by-system report on our bodily functions. Like light, we take health for granted. It is only when the two are gone and the accompanying manifestations of a lack of light or health are evident, that we begin to act. Unfortunately, it is usually in the direction of *alleviating the manifestations* of that lack of health, instead of addressing the cause of it or working to restore the lost health.

What are some of the manifestations of lack of light? The inability to move about confidently without harm is one. How many of us have banged our toe into a dresser or chair in a darkened bedroom in the middle of the night? What should we do? If we are cause/entity oriented, we turn on a light. If we are effects/non-entity oriented, we grope along like a blind person taking small, slow steps. Granted, we may treat the effects because our spouse is sound asleep, but we recognize that the better approach is to turn on the light. Fear is another manifestation of the darkness. A small child will be afraid of the dark at bedtime. It is an unfounded fear. You can explain to the child that he or she is as safe as could be tucked in bed, but reason is usually not a satisfactory method of dealing with the child's fears. A 7.5-watt night light is invariably the answer. A small little bulb fills the void with sufficient light to dispel the manifestations of a lack of light and its symptom, the fear.

Health is the entity, something to be attained. Or perhaps more technically, life is the entity. Life and health are in a sense synonymous terms. We have been able to measure the absolute aspect of life. Science can determine with a fairly good degree of certainty if a person is alive or dead. But we have not yet developed the technology to measure the relative aspect of life, what we call "health." We acknowledge it with such phrases as, "he is not experiencing life to the fullest" or the "quality of life," or "his life is slipping away." What we are alluding to is that life is the entity. A full complement of life is total physical, spiritual, mental and emotional health. It can be lost, to a degree or totally. When it is lost totally, we describe that person as dead because they manifest certain signs and symptoms. Years ago, the lack of a heart beat or the absence of breathing were the manifestations of a lack of life. The medical/legal community more recently has come to the conclusion that a person can be dead before these signs appear, and even "brought back" after they have appeared. Whatever the exact point, at some time an absence of life occurs and eventually that absence of life manifests signs. It also happens on a relative level. At some time an absence of health occurs in individuals and eventually that void manifests signs and symptoms which are referred to as "disease." Just as a person can be pronounced dead while certain functions continue, a person can be partially dead (lacking health) while appearing to be perfectly normal.

•   •   •   •   •   •   •   •   •   •   •   •

Two Approaches to Health

Throughout history, all approaches to the physical well-being of members of the human race have fallen into two general categories that reflect what we are going to call the ADIO (health restoration) and the OIBU (disease treatment) philosophies of life and health, which are health-restoring and disease-treating.

ADIO (Above-down-inside-out)

This acronym represents the health-restoration approach. It acknowledges that health is the result of a power or principle greater than or "above" our finite, educated mind. It also understands that the physical manifestation of this principle in the human organism, the electrical energy of the nervous system, flows over the nerves from the brain "above" -"down" the spinal cord and "outward" to all parts.

OIBU (Outside-in-below-up)

This acronym represents the contrasting or disease-treatment approach. It attempts to control the body and its function or malfunction from the outside. Those that practice this approach believe that an educated mind is better equipped to run the body than the principle that created it. While they may not admit this, their actions bespeak an outside-in viewpoint. Let's look at how these approaches contrast. We will look at OIBU first, since it is the most common approach.

Disease Treatment (OIBU)

In the disease-treatment approach, the symptoms or effects of the disease are treated while the body either gets well from the condition or does not, depending upon the

• • • • • • • • • • • • •

body's inherent ability. For example, an individual suffering with the common cold will be treated for its effects -runny nose, sneezing, coughing, low grade fever, etc. Eventually, the body will rid itself of the virus or bacteria and/or at least reduce its effect by raising the resistance of the tissues to the degree that the disease either no longer manifests itself as symptoms or is no longer present. The treatment of the symptoms have been primarily directed toward making the patient comfortable until the body cured the disease. This approach is especially effective in minor self-limiting conditions like the common cold just mentioned. The practice of medicine is the most well-known discipline directing its efforts in the disease-treatment approach. Much of its practice has been confined to the alleviation of symptoms until the healing process takes place. Pain-killing drugs are probably the most widely used treatment in this aspect of medical practice.

As the practice of medicine has become more technical and advanced, particularly in the latter half of the twentieth century, attention has been directed more toward treating the *cause* of a disease, or the most evident cause (which is usually the last to appear) rather than just confining efforts toward alleviating symptoms. The ultimate example of this effort is demonstrated by the practice of surgery. For example, the most evident cause of gall bladder pain is a malfunctioning gall bladder. Rather than medicate to relieve the pain, the offending organ, unarguably a cause of the pain, is removed. This aspect of the disease-treatment approach has achieved the most dramatic results, but is not without its limitations. One can live without a gall bladder, although,

•   •   •   •   •   •   •   •   •   •   •   •

not as well as with one. The brain, liver, and heart present a greater challenge. Medicine has been working diligently toward meeting that challenge. As a result, some very dramatic accomplishments have been seen. Heart transplants, liver transplants, and kidney transplants are examples. In the disease-treatment approach, continued success is largely dependent upon advances in technology. This works out well in a technological age and in a society that is enamored with continual technical advances. Of course, the down side of this approach is the fact that technology and its accompanying research has a high cost. This creates an economic burden on much of the world, a burden that most cannot bear. Even in a country as affluent as the United States, the cost of disease-treatment technology is growing far faster than the average American's income so that it becomes largely unaffordable. If medicine is to progress in its battle to overcome disease, it must constantly have more sophisticated and greater numbers of weapons to do battle with disease; just as a military establishment must have greater and greater weapons to secure victory on the battlefield.

> The cost of disease treatment technology is growing far faster than the average person's income

Let us now compare the philosophy of the disease-treatment approach with the health-restoration approach.

If we are ever to experience abundant health and end the frustration of fighting diseases, we must begin to look at health and disease from a different perspective.

• • • • • • • • • • • •

Health Restoration (ADIO)

Presently, the accepted world view is that disease is an entity, something to be covered up, negated, destroyed or cut out. That is essentially the medical objective. Health is viewed as an absence of disease, rather than disease being seen as the absence of health. When the disease is removed or eliminated, a void is left which they call "health."

Until we view *health as the entity* which can be created, enhanced, increased, decreased, destroyed or lost, and realize that disease is merely an absence of health, that symptoms are manifestations of that absence, we will never experience our full potential in life.

The Bucket

Let's look at an analogy. Our body is like a large bucket, a health and life container, if you will. Health is like the contents of the bucket (see illustration). By eating properly, getting the proper rest, exercising regularly, maintaining a positive mental attitude, and attending to the other health-promoting measures, we are adding to the contents of the bucket. Reduce any one of them and you diminish the level of health. They all add to the level. No single one of them assures health. But together they combine to fill our body (the bucket) with health. We can diminish the flow into the bucket by diminishing the amount being added. There is also a maximum limit that we can add of each component of health. They are like faucets. There is a maximum flow. There is a sufficient diet. Any more doesn't add to it. More exercise than is necessary does not increase the flow into the bucket. Getting more rest than you need does not increase the flow. In fact, too much of the above can have a detri-

• • • • • • • • • • • •

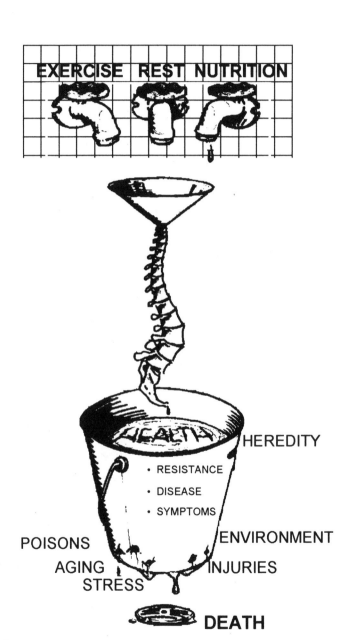

mental effect upon the body, just as too much hot water in your morning shower will burn you. Stress is the result of trying to force open the faucet more than its maximum capacity. That stress may be in the form of too much food or too much exercise. But if we continually add the maximum of each component, we can expect a lifetime of health.

You would think that constantly adding to the contents, constantly adding to health, would cause the bucket to overflow in a short period of time. Life would be great if we all "overflowed with health." Unfortunately, the problem with our bucket is that it has some holes in it. Through these holes leak the contents of the bucket. The first and most important hole is near the top. This is the hereditary factor. Actually, it is at a different level for everyone. It is like the hole at the top of the bathroom sink to prevent it from running over. Each one of us has been given a genetic potential for health, a level that we can reach, established by our genetic makeup. It has been said, if you want to be healthy, first choose your grandparents wisely. Each of us has a level of health we can reach and for each it is different. That may be one reason why some people who appear to take care of their health die at age 60 while others who obviously do not, live to be 100. Our objective in life, relative to health, should be to reach our potential. Probably very few ever attain their genetic health potential. One thing is sure, none of us are going to pass it. But it is not the hole at the top of the bucket that contributes to most people's demise. We lose our health through the holes in the bottom of the bucket. We continually deplete our health; hence the need to continually replenish the volume. The holes are caused by the stress of

•   •   •   •   •   •   •   •   •   •   •   •

life, by the pollutants in our environment, by the poisons we take into our bodies in the form of additives, preservatives, and other chemicals in our food and water. The aging process itself robs the body of some of its health. Some of the holes can be repaired to a greater or lesser degree. How large the holes are will determine to a degree the level of health. The larger the holes, the more conscious we must be about "adding" to our health level. Unfortunately, those people who seem to have the greatest number and the largest leaks in their bucket, for some reason do not have or take the time to concentrate on refilling the bucket. Often patients will say to me, "I know I should come in more regularly for care, but I'm just so busy with..." and then they tell about their two jobs, civic, church and family responsibilities, the softball team, the yardwork, and the list goes on. The person who does not have the time to exercise regularly is the person who needs it the most. You cannot have health "leaking" out the holes without replenishing the supply just as quickly. For if you allow your health to be drained off without refilling it, disease is the result.

Disease is merely a manifestation that your health is being reduced to dangerous levels. When our health volume is reduced, either from creating new holes, failing to close off or at least minimize the size of those we can and failing to replenish the health level at a sufficient rate, disease is a manifestation. The first manifestation is lowered resistance, reduced potential and then warnings from the body that a

• • • • • • • • • • • • •

dangerous volume drop is occurring. Unfortunately, most human beings have developed the ability to ignore these warnings, either by not paying attention to the body's warning systems or by covering them up with over-the-counter drugs. Those warnings may include just not feeling good, sluggishness, non-specific symptoms, tiredness and irritability. We have all experienced them for one reason or another, from time to time. It is the body's early warning system that dangerous levels are being reached. The oil light on your dashboard says that your oil level is low, and if not increased, the engine may experience severe and costly damage. Why do we pay attention to the warning light on a car telling us the oil level is low, but ignore the signs that our body's health level is low? The level continues to decrease until disease results. The cause of the disease is a low health level in the body. The reduction in the health level may be related to the specific aspects of health that have been ignored, such as insufficient diet, lack of rest or exercise or any combination of the above. The signs and symptoms of a particular disease will depend upon which aspect or aspects of health are most lacking. For example, if your diet is insufficient, the disease manifestation may be associated with a lowered resistance due to lack of vitamins and minerals. Your nutrition faucet is merely dripping into your bucket! What goes INTO your bucket constitutes primary and secondary causes of health. The holes in the bucket are the last causes to appear, or tertiary (third level) causes. In this example, the tertiary causes could be micro-organisms (bacteria and viruses) in the environment. Sadly, the practice of medicine has been and continues to be addressing the tertiary factors with first aid. Medicine puts Band-Aids over the holes in the bucket. Depending upon the size of the hole, the number of holes and the effectiveness of the bandage, the holes may be plugged up for a short or long time. The individual, with the leakage temporarily stopped, will continue to add, probably with little effort, to his health level. The level will rise sufficiently to pass the disease manifestation level, and the person then thinks the Band-Aid got him well. Usually this addition is in the form of getting more rest and improving the diet. For some reason, being sick usually forces us to go to bed and to eat better. Antibiotics are a good example of putting a Band-Aid over the hole. Bacteria in the environment create a hole in our bucket, a negative to our health. But as long as we are doing those things necessary to keep our health level above the "resistance" mark, we are fine. When it drops due to lack of rest, poor eating habits, lack of exercise, or whatever reason(s), the manifestation of lack of health that we call disease, occurs. The medical doctor uses the antibiotic as a Band-Aid, the level rises and we get well thinking it was the antibiotic that cured us. It merely slowed the loss of health (by inhibiting bacterial growth) while the individual restored more health by probably taking better care of himself. The Band-Aid is only a short-term fix and eventually the disease will return unless the person concentrates on keeping the health level high. If the level is not kept high, the person's health level will again be reduced to the disease mark. Depending on secondary or tertiary causes, then the same or a different manifestation (different disease) will occur when the disease level is reached.

•   •   •   •   •   •   •   •   •   •   •   •   •

If a person goes through life continually draining off health without replenishing it, the bucket will eventually be empty. We have come to believe that it is a disease that eventually "does us in." Often we think it is one that has "caught us" unaware, without any indication of its presence, like a heart attack or a malignant cancer. The real fact is that we have spent years and years draining off the health from our body without adequately restoring it. When the bucket eventually empties, we die. The attending physician writes on the death certificate as the cause, whatever was manifesting itself at the end. What he should be writing on the certificate is "died due to ignoring health-depleting factors throughout his entire lifetime and by failing to adequately replenish his health level." I doubt that the above will appear on a death certificate in the near future!

Finding the Answers

If we are to experience real health we must understand the above and we must be able to apply this above-down-inside-out thinking to the real-life issue of addressing health-raising measures and health-depleting measures.

This book presents health in a different light, in a way most people may never have thought about. It would be easy to say that everything you ever learned about health is wrong and *Enhance Your Life Experience* is going to tell you what is right. That might have been the best way to market this book and tempt more people to buy it, but that would not be honest. It is true that you have probably been taught many incorrect things over the years but the majority of what you have been taught is true. However, while true, the information you have received has largely been incomplete and that presents a real problem. The instructions for building a model airplane may be accurate in every detail but if steps 7, 12, 15, 18-22 and 27 are missing, only a good deal of luck will prevent your B-29 from looking like something the Wright brothers flew. Incomplete information has been one of the biggest problems with health care in the world for the past one hundred years. People simply have not had all the information they needed to make intelligent decisions regarding their health. Without all of the information, we are in trouble. Part of the problem has been a lack of available information. The human body is probably the most studied piece of "machinery" in the entire world and yet remains one of the least understood. While it is true that more and more is being learned every day, some authorities estimate that we know less than 1/10 of 1% of what there is to know about human physiology. As a result we have been guessing as to what to do in steps 7, 12, 15....

This book is not intended to be an instruction manual to fill in the missing steps. It would be the height of arrogance to presume that one has all the answers to life and health when thousands of books have been written on the subject already, all of which have failed to have any appreciable effect upon the level of health in the world. While that information and knowledge is somewhere for any of us to find, it is not in the following pages. The purpose of this book is to help people recognize the truth when they see it, to separate the truth from the error. The intent of the book is

•   •   •   •   •   •   •   •   •   •   •   •

to give you an outlook, a way of seeing and thinking that will enable you to discern truth from error, half truths from the whole truth and to fill in the blanks for your life and health. We have called this outlook the "above-down inside-out viewpoint" or "ADIO." As you read on, you will learn more about this viewpoint, which sounds strange to you now but will hopefully, make great sense to you by the end of the book. There are answers to just about every health problem and question that confront members of the human race. They are there if you know where to look and how to recognize them when you see them. The problem is that all the answers are not for everybody. That is one of the problems with most approaches to health care. You are asked to believe that the same approach should be used for everybody under all circumstances. That everyone needs X mg of a particular substance, that everyone should adhere to a certain exercise program and everybody needs to drink eight glasses of water every day. Every program is not for everybody at all times. Some are right for you and some are not. Ironically, most of the answers can be found within your own self. Have you ever had someone explain something to you and you say "I should have known that" or "I knew that, I just didn't realize it was the correct answer." Hopefully, that will be your response to many of the concepts in this book.

Writers of books about health generally believe that they have all the answers. This book is different. I am telling you

> The intent of this book is to enable you to discern truth from error for your life and health.

•   •   •   •   •   •   •   •   •   •   •   •   •

I not only don't have all the answers, I don't have any of the answers. What I am presenting is a life and health view that, if understood, can provide you with the ability to find the answers YOURSELF. Every student going through school would like to be given all the answers for every quiz, test and examination. Fortunately, teachers know that is not what education is about. They may give you a few answers as examples but the real key to learning is to understand concepts and principles and be able to apply them to situations, questions and problems. That is true learning, that is what we are about to do. Let's learn about health.

• • • • • • • • • • • •

4

HOW
DO YOU
LOOK AT LIFE?

Time for another test:

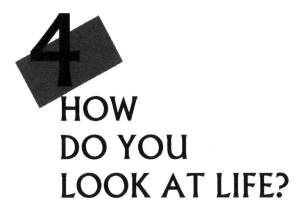

1. Do you believe that the common cold is caused by a virus?

2. Do you believe that ragweed pollen causes hay fever?

3. Do you believe that fluoridation prevents cavities?

4. Do you believe that vaccinations make you healthier?

5. Do you believe that antibiotics will cure the flu?

If you answered "yes" to any of the above questions, you probably have an outside-in viewpoint of life (OIBU) rather than an above-down-inside-out viewpoint (ADIO), at least with regard to matters of health.

Let's look at these viewpoints more closely. There are

basically two general views of the world and life. They are given various names. In science they are called "vitalistic" and "mechanistic," in theology they are called "divine" and "human," and in health we will call them "above-down inside-out" and "outside-in below-up" views. These world and life views are usually established by our culture, our education, our religion, those authority figures who have influenced us in formative years (parents, teachers, coaches, clergy) and by our ability and desire to think in a logical, deductive manner. An individual's world and life view in turn influences his/her thinking with regard to everything including, but not limited to, politics, theology, psychology, sociology and our area of concern, health. It would be interesting to compare the two world and life views in all of the areas listed above but time, space and the subject of this book cause us to confine our discussion to the subject of health and disease and how our view affects our life experience.

The First Disagreement

There are some basic principles with which we can easily contrast the above-down inside-out and the outside-in below- up world and life view. The first involves the recognition of a higher power, an Intelligence or Being that is greater and smarter than the finite mind of man. For our discussion, that higher power is viewed as a law or principle of organization and referred to as universal intelligence. This is not to deny or detract from the theological above-down inside-out world view of a Being. In theology or religion the recognition of this higher power is personified (God) and worshipped. Health care systems are not religious in nature but often share the common truth of recognizing a higher power. For our purposes it is sufficient to acknowledge it as a principle or law.

ADIO

The ADIO viewpoint recognizes that it is this principle of organization that holds the world together, organizing everything from the atom to the galaxies. The principle itself is the major premise of an above-down inside-out health philosophy. If this principle of organization is universal, then it exists in all living matter, including human beings, organizing each of us as well as the planets whirling through space.

To differentiate this principle being expressed in living matter from that in non-living matter we call that which is found in living things "innate intelligence." In reasoning with an above-down inside-out perspective one can say that if this intelligence exists and it is above our finite, educated mind, then *it* should run the body. Or, as it has once been said, "innate intelligence is smart, I'm not." In actuality, the person who said that is a very bright man. He is smart enough to realize that his education is nothing in comparison to the principle of life called "innate intelligence." No matter how smart we are, no matter how much education we have, we could not build even one living, human cell. Yet the human body makes 300 million every minute. Recognition of a greater wisdom than ourselves is the basic principle of the above-down inside-out world and life viewpoint.

● ● ● ● ● ● ● ● ● ● ● ● ●

OIBU

The contrasting outside-in world view is that there is no wisdom or power greater than the educated mind of mankind. This view considers mankind and the educated mind to be the center of the universe. This philosophy does, however, recognize the self-evident fact that often the educated mind makes wrong decisions and is involved in wrong actions. But that, they say, is because the educated brain is either not educated enough or is still evolving to a higher level. This world view believes that the educated brain has the ability, the right and the duty to run, control, heal and cure the human organism. It maintains that life is merely a chemical experiment and that there is no vitalistic phenomena controlling the life process. "Vitalism" is the belief that the processes of life cannot be explained by the laws of physics and chemistry alone, that there is some self-determining aspect of life. Without the recognition of a vitalistic phenomena it is up to man to "mix the chemicals" in the human organism to bring about the desired results. They believe that one day, given enough education, they will mix the chemicals in just the right manner to make and keep people healthy and even create a living organism.

The most well-known spokesman for the Outside-In philosophy was Karl Marx

Vitalism, on the other hand, is the recognition that there is a non-material phenomena that is a fundamental part of life. Vitalism is a basic tenet of the above-down inside-out world view. It holds that there is something apart from chemicals and matter that gives life to them. Something above our understanding or ability to empirically (with the senses) identify. The contrasting tenet of the outside-in below-up viewpoint, that man is merely a machine and all functions can be explained in terms of physics and chemistry alone, is called "mechanism". This viewpoint, of course, also believes society as a whole can be controlled and manipulated for the good of whoever is most educated or in power (in the case of applying the outside-in viewpoint to political philosophy). The most well known spokesman of this philosophy was Karl Marx and his followers. They viewed man as just a machine, treated him as such and relegated him to the junk heap when his usefulness had been served.

If life is merely physics and chemistry in action and the educated brain is the highest authority and wisdom, then there is nothing wrong with altering, changing or destroying parts or all of the organism. Nothing has more right or greater ability to do it than the educated mind of man, and especially a mind that has been educated for eight to ten years longer than everyone else's minds. These contrasting principles are perhaps the greatest indication of the gulf that exists between the practice of above-down inside-out, vitalistic health care and the outside-in below-up, mechanistic approach, i.e., the practice of medicine.

Perhaps it should be stated here that this is not an indictment upon the outside-in below-up approach. As we will see shortly there is a time and place for the outside-in approach as long as it is understood for what it is, that it is limited in its value and effectiveness and that it is definitely not an approach to HEALTH. A Band-Aid may be necessary

● ● ● ● ● ● ● ● ● ● ● ● ●

for a cut finger but nobody mistakenly believes that adhesive bandages heal cuts. Further, there are probably some members of all of the different health professions who have an above-down inside-out world and life view just as there are others with the outside-in below-up viewpoint. What we are dealing with here is not a particular profession or even the individual practice but the principles or philosophy behind these practices.

It is also a fact that on occasions we may think or act inconsistently with our world and life view. That is understandable and expected. It is not right but we are not perfect. There are many who will profess an ADIO philosophy and worship a Being greater than themselves on Sunday in church, but who answered "yes" to some or all of the questions at the beginning of this chapter. The important thing is to recognize when we have done it and then make the necessary adjustments. Of course, when we continually act in a manner that is inconsistent with our world view, it is time to reexamine our thinking. If we do not apply our world and life view to every aspect of our lives we must seriously consider that viewpoint. The doctor who espouses a philosophy that is above-down inside-out in nature, but becomes an authority for the patient on matters that are strictly the function of the patient's innate intelligence needs to re-evaluate his actions. He is little better than the medical physician who claims to have an above-down inside-out philosophy of life because he goes to church on Sunday but does not in any way acknowledge the innate intelligence of the body and its superior ability to run the patient's body. There is no practical application to his supposed view of life.

•   •   •   •   •   •   •   •   •   •   •   •   •

There is no logical outworking of his above-down inside-out philosophy six days a week.

As mentioned, we all occasionally do things that are inconsistent with our world and life view. Some-times we do not think

> We may be thinking or acting inconsistently with our world and life view

enough about an action to realize it is inconsistent. Some-times we do not think about the ramifications of an action. Sometimes we desire to help people. This is particularly true in using procedures that, while pain-relieving, do more harm than good because they are an outside-in approach. Doctors too frequently prescribing medication to relieve symptoms of a condition while the condition itself becomes life-threatening and its cause is ignored is a good example. Sometimes we are selfish and sometimes there is insufficient time to run it through our norms and standards. Often after the situation or incident has passed we say "now why did I do that?" All these situations will happen to us occasionally. But when we act inconsistently with what we claim is our world and life view day in and day out, there is something radically wrong.

Perhaps the major problem with all of us is that we do not examine the motivation or the basis for our actions, even something as simple as taking an aspirin. Millions are consumed every day without as much as a conscious thought. People will take their car to the mechanic the minute they hear an unusual sound coming from under the hood. They want to know the cause and correct it. They know that if they ignore it, there may be costly consequences. Yet many will take an aspirin, in a sense ignoring their pain and its underlying cause, without a second thought. Looking for cause is an above-down inside-out approach, treating symptoms is outside-in below-up. If your view is that there is a higher power that controls and runs the universe, then your life should reflect that principle, every day and in every way. You should seek to involve that principle in everything you do, including your health. Not as a last resort or as a passive observer, but as the major participant in the process. Years ago I watched a television series called "Ben Casey, M.D." In one episode he walked out of surgery, sweaty and worn out, and came face to face with the parents of a child upon which he has just operated. Of course, they ask the question that was tormenting them: "Will our little boy be all right, Dr. Casey?" He tenderly and softly responded, "We have done all that we can do, it is now up to another Power." That pretty much sums up the difference between the philosophy of outside-in doctors and above-down doctors. The one utilizes the greater power as a last resort after he has done all he can. The other acknowledges and utilizes this greater power from the start, builds his health care around it, tries only to remove interference to its expression and intervenes as a last resort.

The Second Disagreement

ADIO: Man's physical problems are caused by internal factors.

OIBU: Man's physical problems are caused by external factors.

The above-down inside-out world and life view says that the cause comes from within. Something is wrong with the individual that causes him or her to begin to lose their health and eventually manifest disease symptoms. This view looks within for the cause. The medical field generally sees the cause as coming from outside the organism. They maintain that germs cause disease, ragweed pollen causes hay-fever, smoking causes cancer, cholesterol causes heart disease. Most people believe this idea. Often even those who think they have an above-down inside-out viewpoint accept it. However, once someone explains to these people why these factors are *not* the cause many who have an above-down inside-out viewpoint of life say, "How could I have been so stupid as to believe that?!"

The problem is that we often accept the words of an authority over our own world viewpoint, despite the fact that it is inconsistent with our understanding. If the reader learns nothing else from this book it should be, accept none of this book on the basis of authority. Develop a reasonable, rational viewpoint and then filter everything through that viewpoint. If it is consistent, accept it. If not, reject it. Of course, if you find too many things that make sense and are inconsistent with your viewpoint, then perhaps you should change your viewpoint.

Germs, pollen, smoking and cholesterol are perfect examples of how we may fail to utilize our philosophy in all aspects of our life. It is true they all are factors in disease, but only influencing or tertiary factors (of third importance). To say they are the cause is a half truth and a half truth is not the truth. In fact, it is as bad as a lie when it causes incorrect action. Think about it. If ragweed pollen caused hay fever,

•　•　•　•　•　•　•　•　•　•　•　•

everybody would have hay fever. We all breathe in the ragweed pollen. Obviously, hay fever is caused by a body that is not producing a chemical necessary to neutralize the pollen and adapt the body to it. Those people whose bodies produce that chemical in sufficient quantity never have hay fever. Those that produce it fairly well are only bothered when the pollen count gets exceptionally high, higher than their body can handle. The degree that the body produces the chemical will determine the severity of the symptoms or the presence of the disease at all.

Perhaps taking an antihistamine (an outside treatment) to relieve the symptoms of hay fever does not seem like such a major issue. But suppose the chemical not being produced is also a necessary part of the immune system or important in the prevention of cancer. Treating the symptom and ignoring the need to get the body working again (correcting the inside problem) has more ramifications than just the side effects of the drug. (Although it is worth noting that people have died in auto accidents from the effects of antihistamines, causing drowsiness and delayed reaction time.)

Germs Are Not Our Enemies

Germs do not attack healthy people. This is obvious simply by the constant presence of germs in our lives. If germs alone caused disease, we would all be sick. The resistance of an individual (internal cause) must be lowered before the germ (outside influencing factor) "makes you sick."

The smoking/cancer issue is also quite interesting and is even being debated within the medical/legal community. I suspect that the discussion is based on economics rather than philosophical viewpoint. The doctors and lawyers for the tobacco industry contend that it has not been clearly demonstrated whether smoking causes cancer. Apparently, many of the millions of people who have never smoked have been diagnosed with cancer, while many heavy smokers have not.

Smoking is certainly not good for one's health. There is no argument about that. Neither is sticking your nose in the exhaust pipe of a city bus. But we must differentiate between common sense

> We cannot blame sickness and disease on these external influencing factors alone

health measures and believing that influencing factors are the cause of disease.

It is not intelligent to inhale poison of any kind. It is not good hygiene to allow people to cough and sneeze in your face. It is not in the best interest of your health to eat greater amounts of red meat than your body needs. But we must not blame sickness and disease on these external influencing factors alone. You may be thinking at this point, "what difference does all this make?" There is a big difference whether we address our attention toward influencing external factors or internal causes; it is more than just a matter of words. Addressing internal causes is crucial for many reasons.

First, there are more influencing factors than one could ever hope to eliminate. Germs (bacteria and viruses) are perfect examples. They are a normal part of our environment. Medical science has spent millions of dollars trying to develop drugs to eliminate them. Yet they are still with us. In fact, in our attempts to rid ourselves of them, we have actually created super germs, those that are resistant to our drugs. It seems that germs have an innate intelligence of their own and are able to adapt to the "poisons" that we try to use on them. As far as hay fever is concerned, there is more pollen in the air than we can ever hope to eliminate.

2 Addressing internal causes is also necessary because when we blame disease on external, influencing factors, we confuse the issue as to what is normally taken into the body (pollen, germs and cholesterol) and what is abnormal (cigarette smoke). All are lumped together as bad. Yet the former all serve a necessary function for human beings. Having an above-down inside-out philosophy which is primarily common sense, helps one distinguish the good, external, influencing factors from the bad. Research, with an outside-in below-up philosophy, seems to be addressing its attention toward treating the external, influencing factors rather than searching for and eliminating internal causes. While it may be beneficial for the Surgeon General to warn us of the damages of cigarette smoke, the attitude it creates causes more harm than good. Money is spent on disease-treating research rather than health- promoting research. Medical costs and disease care costs are escalating at a tremendous rate and have become one of the major issues in society. Yet, very little research effort or money is spent with an above-down inside-out viewpoint in mind.

3 Third, there are great dangers, in the form of side effects, in addressing the influencing factors rather than correcting internal causes. People get sick and die from antibiotic therapy. No one has ever died from eliminating the internal cause, for example, lowered resistance. Raising a person's resistance has no negative side effects. Drugs to treat hayfever allergies have harmful side effects. I often wonder how many industrial accidents occur because of the drowsiness or delayed reaction caused by these drugs. You would not want to get on an airplane with a pilot who has been drinking alcohol. Yet dozens of pilots everyday are flying airplanes having taken medication that has exactly the same or even worse effects than alcohol. Getting the body to work better so that it produces the necessary chemicals itself (the internal cause) can only have positive results. People with pollen allergies often get well because when the internal causes, such as chemical imbalances caused by nerve interference, are removed, the body begins to work better. It often works well enough to produce the needed chemicals during the allergy season and the individual does not develop symptoms. But even in those cases where the person, due to limitations within the body, does develop the symptoms of allergies, they still have a better functioning body. A body with allergies and a good nerve supply is better off than a body with allergies and a poor nerve supply. A body with allergies and good eating habits is better off than one with poor eating habits. The same holds true for exercise and rest. People who are under true "health" care may get well suddenly but is that the only "side effect"? As they improve their health, their allergies disappear. The person may begin to exercise for health reasons and find that his or her headaches disappear. They may begin to eat well and

•   •   •   •   •   •   •   •   •   •   •   •

find their sleeping habits improve. Increasing your health has widespread positive ramifications.

4 The fourth danger is quite simple. In addressing influencing factors, you are essentially treating effects and neglecting cause. A very great danger to the outside-in philosophy is that it sends people searching for truth in the wrong direction. Outside-in thinking has promoted outside-in treatment for the last one hundred years. The approach of many doctors generally has been that disease comes from the outside and therefore the cure must come from the outside. They believe they must develop stronger, more powerful substances to put into the body to fight more powerful and threatening diseases. In the middle ages people lived in fear of the plague. Today people live in fear of AIDS. Not much progress in seven hundred years!

5 The fifth danger, and perhaps the greatest, is that outside-in thinking promotes irresponsibility in people when it comes to matters of health. That has prompted the writing of this book. If people believe that the cause of their problem (in this discussion we are dealing specifically with physical problems but the discussion could be applied to all sorts of problems) comes from outside, they can easily be vindicated of any blame or responsibility on their part to take care of themselves so that they will maintain a high level of resistance. Man has always tried to blame someone or something for his failings. Adam blamed Eve, and Eve said, "the Devil made me do it!" Disease was thought to be caused by demons, darkness, leaving your windows open at night and even bathing. It is easy to foist responsibility on someone or something else. The latest is claiming weight

• • • • • • • • • • • •

problems are due to heredity, putting the responsibility on the parents. While there may be genetic factors which predispose some of us toward weight problems, each of us must take responsibility for ourselves. Even people who choose to smoke for years want to blame the tobacco industry for their cancer. People do not want to take responsibility for their problems.

The outside-in philosophy gives them a perfect excuse. It gets them off the hook as far as responsibility and as far as doing something about it. The medical field, when it maintains that the cause is outside and the cure is outside, contributes to that irresponsibility. People have angioplasty procedures to open their arteries. That is the procedure where a little balloon is inflated in the artery that has been blocked. The medical profession itself is in disagreement over the value of the procedure. But too many people believe that if the arteries close up again following the procedure they will simply have it done again. People are having by-pass surgery two and three times. Obviously, they do not see the need to seriously do something about their arteries, such as, developing health habits e.g., eating well, exercise, health maintenance. People, more than anything, need to begin to take responsibility for their health, to begin to realize that health comes from within. As long as they are told that the cause is

> "When man violates man's laws, we send him to jail and point the finger of scorn at him. When he violates nature's laws, we send him to a hospital, give him flowers and feel sorry for him."

outside and the cure is outside they will consider themselves a victim of their circumstances and never assume respon-

• • • • • • • • • • • • •

sibility for their health. B.J. Palmer, the developer of chiropractic once said, "When man violates man's laws, we send him to jail and point the finger of scorn at him. When he violates nature's laws, we send him to a hospital, give him flowers and feel sorry for him."

There is a fairly new term in the area of psychology and interpersonal relations. It was undoubtedly coined by someone with an above-down inside-out philosophy. The term is "enabling." It means allowing and encouraging irresponsible and often self-destructive behavior in others by shielding them from the consequences of their actions. It paves the way to make more and more unhealthy choices. The outside-in below-up philosophy is an enabling one. We have antacids and other remedies for people who overeat or eat the wrong foods thereby encouraging irresponsible eating habits and discouraging people with digestive disorders to find out why their bodies cannot tolerate certain normal foods. We have pain killers and headache remedies to encourage abusing our bodies. Wake up pills and sleeping pills that encourage poor sleeping habits. Lotions, balms and ointments to encourage abusing our muscles. The list is almost endless and it keeps increasing. Medical technology contributes to the problem. The success of organ transplants, although extremely limited, causes people to begin to view their bodies as they would automobiles with replaceable parts. There is clearly a need in some cases for therapies and for transplants, but they also may encourage irresponsible behavior.

The contrasting viewpoints on the cause of physical problems is the crux of the whole battle between the ADIO and the OIBU viewpoint. It leads to how we approach our life and health. This leads to the third aspect of the conflict.

The Third Disagreement

ADIO: The cure for man's physical problems must come from within.

OIBU: The cure for man's physical problems will come from outside.

The third principle is just a logical outgrowth of the first two. From the above-down inside-out viewpoint it logically follows that if the cause is from within, then the cure must also come from within, from correcting the internal cause. Health comes from allowing the innate intelligence of the body to heal from the inside-out. Healing takes place by the *internal* wisdom creating healthy cells *within* the body to replace sick and damaged ones. New healthy tissue is not introduced into the body from the outside, it is produced within.

True health care professionals who are successful recognize their role in the restoration of health. They play a very humble, very minor role. They do not heal people or cure people. They do not take credit for the so-called "miracles" that are seen every day in their offices. They acknowledge that their procedure does not cure. It merely brings the innate intelligence of the body into right relationship with the physical matter. What occurs after that is strictly a function of the body. It is out of the practitioner's ability to control and may even be beyond his or her ability to comprehend. When doctors, of any kind, set aside that perspective and begin to think they are the healers, their care quickly degenerates into an outside-in therapy.

•   •   •   •   •   •   •   •   •   •   •   •   •

The outside-in tenet that says the cure will come from outside is a logical extension of its philosophy. If there is no wisdom greater than the educated mind of mankind, then it is up to him to find and provide all the answers to mankind's problems. The medical field has had some limited success in treating mankind's problems. The temporary alleviation of diseases and their symptoms have encouraged them to continue their outside-in efforts. They believe that if they can temporarily relieve disease, then it is only a matter of time before they come up with a technique, procedure or drug that will do it for extended periods of time. If you treat the disease long enough, eventually it will not matter any longer. As one outside-in economist once said when questioned about the wisdom of printing money with no gold to back it up, "in the long run we will all be dead anyhow." His thinking is largely responsible for inflation. Let's look at an example of how this thinking addresses a real-life medical problem.

Recently a friend lost his father. He had been a recipient of a heart transplant and had lived five years with the donor heart. There is no doubt that some lives are extended by heart transplants. However, the question is always raised whether the quality of life makes the procedure worthwhile. The recipients and their families are the only ones who have the right to make that judgment! The problem is that the patient and family have no frame of reference to make the decision. Neither does the physician. He does not tell the patient that he will always be sick. That he will always take drugs, spend thousands of dollars a month and eventually, if the heart transplant is a success, surely die of cancer or some other disease because drugs have suppressed the immune system.

•   •   •   •   •   •   •   •   •   •   •   •

The patient is not told those things.

An even greater concern, however, is the one that addresses the world and life viewpoint issue. When medical science began to go in the direction of heart-transplant therapy they did so because of a mindset. The mindset is the outside-in below-up philosophy that says if we put a healthy heart into a sick body we will end up with a healthy body. When in fact, all you end up with is a sick body and a healthy heart which will eventually become sick. You can no more expect a healthy heart to make a sick person healthy than you can expect a freshly picked green apple to make a barrel of rotten apples edible. The field of medicine has spent billions of dollars researching heart transplants and developing the technology to do them. They advertise and promote the procedure, they have waiting lists of people who want them, many of whom will never get them. Yet, they have done virtually nothing to look for the causes of heart disease, why people get sick in the first place and how they can keep people healthy so they do not need heart transplants. That is not a priority of the outside-in thinkers, because in doing that, you must ulti-mately look inside for the cause and that is foreign to their world and life viewpoint.

The outside-in approach wants to spend money researching disease. Unfortunately, they hold the purse strings. The above-down inside-out approach wants to research health. If money was the answer, at least one disease would most certainly be cured by now. Jerry Lewis has raised more money for muscular dystrophy than probably any group has for any other disease. Yet the disease still occurs. With regard to the heart transplant, they are not even working toward finding inside-out procedures that might enable heart- transplant candidates to regain their health. It is assumed and accepted that nothing can be done for these people except transplant surgery. No other measures are taken and consequently, the assumption becomes a self-fulfilled prophecy. The patient is told if they do not get the transplant, they will die. So they are put on a list, and they wait for a donor and basically, do nothing. If they do not get the transplant, they die. There are some exceptions. Some doctors will attempt to raise the health level of some of these heart transplant candidates who don't have access to hearts, by suggesting changes in their diets and exercise. These, however, are the minority who think with an above-down inside-out mindset and it is admittedly difficult to gauge or enforce compliance. The accepted thinking is that the problem will be solved when we have enough donors or produce drugs that can overcome the immune system's normal response of rejecting the donor organ.

There is nothing wrong with a heart transplant if that is what a person wants, being totally informed of the pros, cons and alternatives. It has helped people. But there is something wrong with the *thinking* that gave rise to heart transplants. That thinking comes from an outside-in approach to health. An outside-in approach focuses on disease rather than health. Perhaps we need to look at health and disease in an altogether different light.

If you are not beginning to see the differences between these viewpoints and how the one leads to a health

•   •   •   •   •   •   •   •   •   •   •   •

improving life and the other leaves you waiting to be sick, the remainder of this book will have little value to you. To check your understanding, go back to the questions at the beginning of this chapter.

Does it seem more reasonable that a lack of resistance is a greater cause of the common cold than a virus or bacteria?

Does is seem more logical to get the chemistry of the body in balance than to take allergy medication? If you are starting to question long-standing beliefs, there is hope for you. READ ON!

●   ●   ●   ●   ●   ●   ●   ●   ●   ●   ●   ●

IT IS NOT NECESSARILY NORMAL TO BE AVERAGE!

It is interesting

how two words can so clearly sum up the contrasting philosophies of the world and life views of above-down inside-out and outside-in below-up. The irony is that often the two words are used interchangeably, which unfortunately creates incorrect thinking in people, and incorrect thinking gives rise to incorrect actions.

Average, simply put, is found by dividing the sum total of a set of figures by the number of figures summed. Add together 20, 30, 33, 43, 50 and 60 then divide it by six and your average figure is 39.33. *Normal,* on the other hand, is defined by Webster as "that which is occurring naturally." *Average* is a figure derived from the educated mind of man. *Normal* occurs naturally. *Average* is an artificial figure based upon a numbering system of ten which we have created.

Normal cannot be changed without outside intervention. *Average* can be determined by anyone with the ability to add and divide. *Normal* is determined by the innate intelligence of the body. It varies from moment to moment depending upon the needs of the individual. Let's look at some examples.

Heart Rate

If a man were to run around the block, his heart rate may elevate as high as 120 beats per minute. At that moment the innate intelligence has responded to a particular activity and the need that has been created in the body. It is a perfectly normal response of the body. However, if you were to compare that person's heart rate with someone else, it would be considered above normal because the "normal" (really the average) is approximately 72 beats per minute. But 72 beats per minute is probably *not* normal for a person who has just been running. That may seem to be an extreme example because the heart rate is usually taken at a resting state and the physician taking it surely would not compare someone who has just run around the block with someone who is in a resting state. But the point is that something different was happening to the runner's body creating a different situation and the need for a different heart rate. We would not expect his heart to maintain the "normal" (actually average) 72 beats per minute, because the situation called for something else. What about situations that could occur and create a need for changes in the body that would be departures from the average, but of which the examining physician would have no knowledge? It goes back to a knowledge of the body and frankly, our knowledge of the body is extremely limited.

Body Temperature

The most common example occurs thousands of times in thousands of homes every day. Fever is one of the most misunderstood, adaptive reactions to occur in the human body. Every mother worries about fever because sooner or later almost every child will end up with an elevated temperature. She puts a thermometer in his mouth, one that has a little red line at 98.6 F. Is that figure "normal"? 98.6 is an *average* temperature determined by adding the temperatures of a group and dividing by the number of the group. Mom begins to worry and either starts with cold baths or begins to give aspirin to the child to get his temperature down to what she believes is "normal." But this is not necessarily in the best interest of the child. The *fever* may very well be the normal response of the body.

Until recently doctors viewed fever as a symptom of infection, something that, along with the infection, needed to be treated. Fortunately, some very important research at the University of Michigan changed that. A physiologist conducted an experiment on desert iguanas and found that those who developed an elevated temperature during an infection had a far greater survival rate than those who did not. Iguanas, being cold-blooded animals, cannot raise their own temperature. They must seek out warmer areas to elevate their body temperature. The infected ones that were able to crawl under a heat lamp and raise their body temperature from its usual 101 degrees up to 104 degrees survived at a rate of 75%. Those infected lizards that were denied access to the heat lamp had just the opposite result, 75% died. Fever, rather than being an unwanted result of the infection, is the innate intelligence of the body's normal response, in this case to the presence of certain bacteria or organisms. The research concluded that elevated temperature was one of the most important ways of fighting infection. "Taking aspirin, cold baths or other treatment to reduce fever actually may interfere with the body's natural defenses in fighting germs," said Matthew J. Kluger, the physiologist who conducted the experiment. Dr. Kluger is saying something that those in the health field with an ADIO viewpoint and confidence in the body's ability to heal itself have been saying for years. The doctor went on to say "Fever is not a harmful symptom but an efficient defense mechanism. People would probably be better off if moderate fevers were allowed to run their course."

Some other interesting experiments were also done. Researchers injected aspirin-type drugs, one of the most effective fever-reducing drugs, into the hypothalamus region of rabbits. The hypothalamus is the area in warm-blooded animals largely responsible for the regulation of body temperature. It is the "thermostat" of the body. The results showed that while the aspirin did effectively prevent fever in infected rabbits, most of them unfortunately died.

Scientists have been amazed at the variety of activities that occur during a fever. Interferon, a natural virus-fighting chemical, becomes more efficient. The body produces interferon and when the body's temperature is elevated, it is produced in greater quantities and becomes more efficient.

• • • • • • • • • • • •

White blood cells, the body's main defense against micro-organisms, speed more quickly to fight off infection during a fever. They also become more active. Iron, which many germs thrive on, is withdrawn from the blood and stored in the liver. The body's chemical reaction rate is accelerated during a fever. Fever is a normal response of the innate wisdom of the body to an attack by an outside organism. There are millions of different microscopic organisms in our environment and only a small percentage are a threat to the human body. The reason that there are only a few is that many simply can not thrive at a temperature of approximately 98 degrees. There are others that live and grow best at a temperature of 50 degrees. They live in the soil and would die if placed in the human body. The few that do prefer the temperature of the body are not all associated with disease. Some, like E. Coli, are actually beneficial. They help in the digestive process. Take them out of the digestive tract, however, and they are a threat. The body will take great measures to destroy them, all the measures that were just discussed, including fever.

There are other examples that demonstrate how a lack of knowledge of what is actually occurring in the body could cause one to misunderstand the value of an apparent departure from "normal" (which we have just stated is really a manifestation that the body is working normally under different circumstances). As a teenager I went to a wrestling camp in the Pocono Mountains of Pennsylvania one summer. Part way through the week dozens of other boys and myself began experiencing vomiting and diarrhea. It was obviously not a pleasant situation. Apparently either the food

•   •   •   •   •   •   •   •   •   •   •   •   •

or the water had been contaminated, (they never found out or at least never told us). But all those teenage boys' bodies were trying to get rid of something unwanted in their systems. Tainted food or contaminated water is not normal. Getting rid of it by any means as quickly as possible is normal. The directors of the camp, of course, reacted in an outside-in manner and went out and bought bottles of over-the-counter medication that is supposed to stop diarrhea. Fortunately, everyone got over it despite the "medical treatment." It is truly amazing how the body has the ability to get well so often in spite of the things we do to hinder the healing process.

Vomiting

The sad thing is that often these hindrances are attempts to help the body. If we don't know, perhaps we need to just trust the wisdom of the body. There are situations when the body may not want or need food. If the body is fighting an invasive organism, it needs all its energy and does not need the added work of digesting food. But Mom thinks Junior needs food to "keep up his strength" so she pours chicken soup into him. His body doesn't want it or need it so it gets rid of it. Now she is doubly worried because "he can't keep anything down." No one will die without food for a day or so. An injured or sick animal in the wild will not eat. In these situations, not eating allows the innate intelligence of its body to work better. These are just a few examples of how a lack of knowledge of the body's function can lead us to believe that a perfectly normal process is a deviation from normal and that it needs to be corrected or treated. There may be hundreds of other normal functions going on within the body that we are interfering with in an attempt to bring the body back to an "average" state.

Weight

Another problem with using "normal" and "average" is that we really cannot say what is normal for a particular individual. Body weight is an example. Medical science attempts to establish the normal body weight by computing the average and then conforming everyone to it. We are different and unique human beings. If you divide the total weight of a group of people by the number in the group you will get an average weight. That is probably not the normal weight for more than 10% of the group. By conforming the remainder to that standard you are likely doing harm to their health. It is very likely that there are wide ranges of weight that are healthy for individuals.

Weight is one area where we perhaps use our educated brain in a very incorrect way. We allow fashion to dictate what is "normal." The thin look is in. Consequently, women, and to a lesser degree, men, are purposely losing more weight than is healthy for their bodies, just to be in vogue. Why the look is in is hard to understand. Looking at 17th and 18th century paintings, the beautiful women were much heavier than what is considered beautiful today. The desire for a thin look, often accomplished by periods of starving and bingeing, is extremely harmful to one's health.

The field of medicine has begun to take note of how being overweight is not good and may lead to disease. While that may be correct, there are probably more people who are lowering their health by undernourishing their bodies than there are people who are lowering their health by overeating. That is not an excuse for gluttony. The fact is, the body is better able to handle an excess of food than to handle an insufficient amount. If it is getting too much, there are mechanisms within the body to get rid of the excess. The body can store it as fat and will do so to a limited degree. Only people whose bodies are sick and malfunctioning will end up with an unhealthy amount of adipose tissue (fat). After the body stores what it determines is a sufficient storehouse for possible future use, it will begin to pass the rest on through the digestive system. The body will also raise the metabolism to burn off the excess. When it comes to the body being undernourished, the only effective mechanism the body has to conserve is to lower the metabolic rate. That mechanism however, is limited because it still must carry on the normal activities of life, such as the beating of the heart and respiration. The energy output of the heartbeat in a twenty-four hour period alone is enough to raise three fully-loaded Greyhound buses off the ground. The body needs sufficient fuel to generate that much energy. There are numerous other examples that demonstrate orthodox medicine's inability to distinguish between normal and average.

So then...

There are a few distinguishing differences between "normal" and "average," that, if you understand and apply, can go a long way toward improving your understanding of health and how it relates to you.

●　●　●　●　●　●　●　●　●　●　●　●

1 First, "average" is established by the educated mind. It does not matter whether it is a group of scientists using the most sophisticated scientific equipment or a ten year old with a three dollar calculator, it is still the finite educated mind making the determination. The intent of this book is based upon the premise that the educated mind is finite, fallible, arbitrary and biased and when it comes to establishing bodily functions or norms, leaves much to be desired. Establishing what an individual's blood pressure, heart rate, insulin level, minimum daily requirements or anything else should be is, at best, guesswork and, at worst, deadly. "Normal," on the other hand, is established by the innate intelligence of the body. It is established based upon the needs of the moment, upon lifestyle, habits, circumstances and upon many other factors we have no idea of and possibly never will.

2 The second difference is that "average" is a fixed figure. Any deviation from that fixed standard is considered abnormal and usually invokes some kind of medical treatment which may or may not do more harm than good. If the deviation from this fixed standard truly is abnormal, the medical treatment could be of value. If the deviation is normal for that person, the treatment is definitely not in their best interest. "Normal" is not a fixed figure. The body temperature of an individual probably changes dozens of times in the course of the day. The blood pressure, heart rate, and blood sugar level, as well as many other functions of the body also change many times for an individual during the course of a day. The human body is a dynamic organism. It responds to thousands of external and internal stimuli taking

• • • • • • • • • • • •

place within it and within the environment in which it resides. The medical field largely overlooks this principle of dynamics, primarily because they most often view the body when it has lost much of its dynamism. Dynamics are signs of life and health. When the body has lost or lowered its health, much of the dynamic ability it possesses is no longer manifested. This is often the state the physician sees the body in, and hence he/she often fails to appreciate the dynamics of the human organism.

The third difference between normal and average is the **3**one that really causes us a problem. "Average" is always known. It is known because it is a standard that someone has created and applied to us. Right or wrong, we live with that standard (120/80, 72 beats per minute, 98.6 degrees Fahrenheit). Everyone knows what these figures are - blood pressure, heart rate and body temperature. Probably very few know what they mean. "Normal," on the other hand, is rarely known. I have no idea what my blood pressure, heart rate or body temperature should be at this very moment. The question is, do I trust the innate intelligence of my body or do I try to conform it to a national standard set by finite educated minds?

The fourth difference, (the one that demonstrates the **4**true weakness of using average as a measurement of health) is that the basis for establishing the "average" of anything varies based upon our educated knowledge. Medical science has changed the average for blood sugar level in the last twenty years. There is discussion about the fact that 98.6 may not be the most accurate figure for a "normal" body temperature. As education and knowledge increase, changes

• • • • • • • • • • • •

are made. What was considered a normal body weight thirty years ago has changed. Hopefully, the more that science studies and understands the human body, the more they will realize the fallacy of trying to conform dynamic, living human beings into a preconceived idea of what is normal. At this point, the field of medicine, because of its viewpoint, only changes the figures, which may be better for some people and worse for others. The problem lies, not in the figures, or standard that they set, but in the approach toward setting standards for all people in the first place. Once they realize the futility of this approach they just may begin to look elsewhere, that is, inside the organism, toward its innate intelligence to establish what is normal in the life experience. The only way they can accomplish that is by changing their world and life viewpoint.

If we cannot know what is normal for the body, how do we go about getting our bodies into a normal state and maintaining them there? There are ways to do it. We will begin to explore these ways in the next chapter.

•   •   •   •   •   •   •   •   •   •   •   •

6

ADDING TO THE BUCKET

If we cannot know

what is normal for our body, how can we work toward maximum health and know we are moving in the right direction? There are certain measures we can take to increase our likelihood of being truly healthy and the more we apply these measures, the more our body will tell us when we are straying from the course.

Health-raising measures are important factors in determining our health level. They are natural resources we can give to the body. Almost without exception, we use our educated brain to determine the body's need for these measures and how to best supply that need. Hopefully, that need is based upon being sensitive to the urges of the innate intelligence of the body. Sometimes we refer to it as listening to the innate intelligence of the body. It is really a matter of being aware of your body's needs. The extent of awareness of many people is when they look in the mirror in the morning, they are aware that they are alive! If we are to experience maximum health, we must do better than that. The importance of health-raising measures cannot be overestimated. Every health care measure makes a unique contribution to the person. No one measure is a substitute for any other. Let's look at some health-raising measures and the mechanism by which they raise our health level.

 ## Nutrition/Diet

This measure is the easiest to understand. Everyone can see how putting good food into the body is necessary to increase our health level. Enough pictures of children in third world countries have been on the television to demonstrate clearly how important good food is to our health. The innate intelligence of the body takes the food that we eat and makes it into living tissue. That is the difficult task - making skin, organs and bones out of ham and eggs! The easy job is putting the proper foods into the body so the innate wisdom of the body can make flesh and blood. If we had the job of the innate intelligence of the body, we would not last very long. In fact, we often fail to do even the easy job of giving our bodies the material with which to work.

We need to understand what we mean by the word "diet," taken from the Greek "dietia," meaning way of living. We don't mean a prescribed program of food to lose weight. It is, rather, an eating program that you follow for your entire life. Dieting to lose weight is using food for a therapeutic purpose. It is outside-in. (Eating, like exercise and rest, is a health measure that can also be used for therapeutic purposes, although its value is quite limited when used as a therapy.) People do go on prescribed diets to treat obesity (questionably, a disease). A particular diet may be a health-raising measure as well as a treatment for the obesity. As a treatment, its value is limited and like most treatments, it is only temporary. Usually, the individual will gain weight once again because the treatment (the diet) is abandoned once the condition (obesity) is relieved (the desired weight has been reached). An individual who changes his or her eating habits, along with other health-raising measures, will reach the appropriate weight for his or her body as a result of raising the health level rather than treating disease. That is not to say that medically prescribed diets are not effective treatments for obesity, heart disease, diabetes, and other diseases. It is just that these prescriptive approaches to eating have virtually nothing to do with health. They are approaches to the treatment of disease, (e.g., obesity, diabetes) and as important as that is at times, it is simply not health care as we are presenting it. Further, like any treatment, its value is limited to certain people, and even for those people its value is limited. We are calling upon our inadequate educated intelligence to determine both quantity and quality of food.

Quantity of food is not a problem in most of the United States, except in putting too much food into the body! The quality of the food we eat and how to perceive those needs may very well be one of the most difficult aspects of health care. Knowing what needs you have, at least in quantity, is a little easier, although not by much. The first thing to realize is that three meals a day is a relatively modern idea which is not necessarily important to health. If we are individuals with different needs, then it would seem logical that each of us should not necessarily be conformed to three meals per day. Three meals a day may be perfect for some people, too many for others and not enough for still others. Some readers who like to eat and are having visions of six or seven meals a day are saying, "hey, I like this book!" Don't get too excited. If you are thinking that, you are more likely a candidate for less than three a day or three smaller ones!

> When you conform everyone to a standard, it is the lowest common standard

The outside-in philosophy is to conform everyone to a preconceived standard. Invariably, when you conform everyone to a common standard, it is the lowest common standard. That is why Eastern Europe and the Soviet Union rejected "communism." It forced nearly everyone to live at a lower economic level. The ADIO philosophy says that we should listen to the dictates of our bodies. How often do we eat when we are not even hungry, simply because its "mealtime" or for the social aspect of it? There is nothing wrong with friends socializing over a meal, but don't allow it to get in the way of your health. Don't allow peer pressure to rob you of your health. Obviously, convenience and the necessities of life dictate eating habits to some degree. Perhaps that is why it is such a difficult area in which to be aware of the body's actual needs. Some individuals may benefit by eating smaller portions more often. Some others need to try eating less often. It is difficult, to be sure, but you will never know what your body wants unless you make an educated effort to listen. If it is too much trouble or too inconvenient, you may easily slip back into your old habits. If you do, you must realize that your health level will only be raised to the degree that you do the correct things with regard to diet.

This book is not meant to make being healthy easy, because it is not easy. If being healthy were easy, there would not be so many books on the subject and there would not be so many unhealthy people. Being healthy necessitates work, thought, effort and responsible action. I won't give you a prescription for what you should do with regard to diet, nor any other area of health. First, because there are already too many books doing that. All of them work for someone (perhaps only the author) and none of them work for everybody (we are all uniquely different). Second, I would be depriving you of the learning experience. In this instance, experience truly is the best teacher. Third, it is not consistent with a philosophy that says the individual is the best one to make judgments regarding their health. The more you do it, the better you will get at it. The more you do it, the more your body will let you know when you are not eating in accordance with its desires.

Have you ever walked away from the table with an uncomfortable, stuffed feeling, thinking that you never want to eat again? Anything relating to health should not cause that feeling. You have probably overeaten. It happens to me in restaurants. Portions in most restaurants are probably more than most people need. But you paid for it so you think

•   •   •   •   •   •   •   •   •   •   •   •

that you might as well eat it. You certainly don't want to waste it, especially if you were reared not to waste food. We all like to get our money's worth! Next time you feel comfortably full, stop. Get a doggie bag. Listen to your body. Believe me, you will not hurt the waiter or the chef's feelings. Even if you did, your health is more important than whether they think you liked their meal. Talk about getting your money's worth. You've actually been given two meals for the price of one. I've eaten in restaurants where the doggie bag was enough for two more meals.

It is important also to understand "hunger pangs." They are merely your body telling your educated brain that the stomach is empty. It doesn't mean it has to be filled that minute or even that hour. We are taught to avoid pain at all costs. But "pain" that is merely the body informing you of a situation is not bad. If you feel you need to address this symptom because other symptoms accompany it (e.g., headaches, lightheadedness), then perhaps you are one of those people who needs to eat more but smaller meals over the course of the day. If you do nothing, the hunger pangs stop. Once the message gets through, the sender stops sending. There are many books on the market and authorities that can give you information concerning proper diet. This book is not intended to do that. Its purpose is to teach you how to read those books or listen to those authorities. It is meant to give you a perspective so that when you read something or hear something someone says, you can say "that makes sense" or "that's the dumbest thing I ever heard." Here are a few principles that will help:

•   •   •   •   •   •   •   •   •   •   •   •

1 Remember your objective in establishing eating habits is to try to educatedly eat what the innate intelligence of your body needs and wants.

2 Be wary of authorities who make absolute statements, like never eat something or always eat such and such.

Your body is unique, your needs are unique and they vary from everyone else, as well as from day to day.

3 The portions, calories and number of meals you need will quite probably vary from day to day. Do not become a slave of routine. Be flexible and respond to your body's messages. If I am very active on a given day, my needs will be different than if I am writing at my desk.

4 Don't be misled into thinking that supplements are a substitute for good eating habits. There is no substitute for good food. Taking supplements is outside- in thinking. It supports the idea that man, with his finite mind, can put into a tablet what the body takes from food. It encourages poor eating habits. ("I don't need to worry about eating right, I'll get it in my daily supplement.") Taking dietary supplements is at best second rate nutrition for your body. Do you really want to settle for second best?

5 Learn to recognize the difference between the innate intelligence of the body communicating what the body needs and abnormal cravings caused by addiction or habits. Just like with drugs and alcohol, people can develop an abnormal craving for certain foods. It is either psychological (poor expression of the educated intelligence) or a physiological addiction (a body working incorrectly).

6 There is no food that is bad if prepared correctly and eaten in the right quantity. The body is designed to

• • • • • • • • • • • • •

digest and use all types of food. However, some people, due to limitations of matter or a body not functioning properly, do not handle dairy products or meat for example. Some may be allergic to strawberries or tomatoes. There is nothing wrong with the food, the problem lies with the body. Use good, educated decisions (i.e., common sense) to avoid foods that do not agree with you. Recognize however that the cause is within your body and work toward correcting that cause.

All programs and concepts relating to diet and eating should be liberally sprinkled with common sense.

 ## Rest

Resting the body to improve health is easily understood. People with the flu go to bed to rest and they improve. It is not because the body fights off a virus better in the horizontal position! Fighting the organism is not what gets you well. Raising the health level is. Rest and sleep are health-restoring measures which we need to do every night.

Here are a few principles to understand which will be helpful in meeting your body's rest needs.

1 Each person's needs are different. If this sounds like a repeating theme in this book, it is! One of the most important aspects of the ADIO philosophy, in general, is that each person is an individual and only the innate intelligence of that person's body is capable of knowing what is right for him or her. The best we can do with our educated intelligence is to try to understand what the innate

intelligence is doing, make sure we do not interfere with those actions and remove any interferences to those actions. I am amazed at the wide variations in sleep that different people need. It is said that Thomas Edison got along on a few hours sleep per night. There are other people who simply cannot function properly without at least nine or ten hours per night. Strangely, it appears to have very little to do with whether a person does physical work or mental work. It is also important to note that the same person needs more sleep on certain occasions and less on others. Going to bed after the 11:00 o'clock news every night may be ignoring the innate intelligence of your body and the rest it needs.

2 Listen to your body. Rest is the easiest area of health to get in touch with our body's needs. The more we listen and act accordingly, the easier it will become with regard to this area and all other areas of health. If you feel tired, take a nap. If you do not, go on with your day's activities. Of course, it is very difficult with social and work obligations to follow an "innate response program." Students occasionally came into my 8 a.m. class a half hour late and said that the innate intelligence of their body wanted them to sleep longer. It may have been true but it didn't keep them from being marked "late." The more you get out of educated habits, the easier it will become to follow the dictates of your body; rest is the best way to begin.

3 Sleep where and how you are most comfortable. From a structural, bio-mechanical or orthopedic standpoint, authorities say people should sleep in a particular manner. But the human body is a dynamic organism. Trying to conform its sleeping position to someone else's idea is

• • • • • • • • • • • • •

inconsistent with the ADIO philosophy. Sleep however you are most comfortable. When it comes down to it, you really have very little control over the position in which you sleep. Your educated brain is, for the most part, nonfunctional when you are asleep. So the innate intelligence of the body will move you to whatever position or positions are best throughout the night. The only thing you can do educatedly is put yourself in the position that enables you to fall asleep as quickly as possible.

Exercise

"Exercise is the requisite amount of activity to promote adaptation."

Ralph Stephenson

As a health measure, exercise is another little understood concept. What Stephenson is saying above is that exercise, to be beneficial, is the exact amount of activity to enable the body to better adapt to its environment. No more, no less. We have seen what happens to people who get absolutely no activity. The body literally wastes away. Unfortunately, most people either associate exercise with training for some athletic endeavor or they think of it as a rehabilitation measure (therapy). Others believe that it involves their normal activities in life. Many a patient, when asked if they exercise will say, "I get enough exercise at work." WRONG! While more and more authorities are saying that work constitutes physical exercise, unless your job is as a professional athlete, you are probably not exercising your body totally or giving all of it a sufficient workout.

The human body in "a natural state" probably does not

need an exercise program. When we lived in a hunter/ gatherer or farming society, the need to have an exercise program was probably minimal. With the coming of the industrial revolution, machines began to do the work. Those that did physical work usually performed a repetitive activity, failing to adequately exercise the entire body. With the technological age that we are now in, very few people during the course of a day are getting any, let alone sufficient exercise. Add to that the fact that the major leisure time activity of the American public from school children to retirees is watching television, and it becomes clear why a concerted effort to exercise must be made. We need to use our educated brain in a positive way to compensate for the restrictions and demands that modern society has placed upon us. A painter may spend eight hours a day lifting his arms to paint the walls or with his head bent back to paint ceilings. Consequently, he does not need to exercise certain shoulder, arm and chest muscles. They get more than enough activity. But that does nothing for the cardiovascular system. You need to have a regular program to exercise it. The mailman who walks five to eight miles a day is in just the opposite situation. He needs to exercise muscles, whatever they might be, that are not being exercised by his work. Again a few principles would be helpful to the person trying to use exercise to help raise their health level to its maximum and keep it there.

1 Everyone's exercise needs are different. The mailman, the factory worker and the cab driver all need to exercise, but their needs are unique to them. Each individual should determine the program that is best for him or her. There is probably no area of health where we are more prone and anxious to follow a program prescribed by a "professional." We want someone, especially an authority, to tell us which exercises to do, how many and how often. That is an outside-in approach. There is nothing wrong with using the expertise of people trained in the area of exercise. But remember, no two people on the face of the earth should have the same exercise program. We are all different. A program should reflect our age, body size, lifestyle and every other aspect that is unique to us. Even a "personal trainer," if he or she is a good one, will be responding to the client's input to set up a program. Ideally, the client's input should be in response to the body's messages.

2 No exercise program should be fixed in stone. I like routine, perhaps more than most people. Exercise should be a part of our daily routine. But the exercises we do should show a certain degree of flexibility. On a day that I play tennis, I do not need to jog. As our lifestyle changes (e.g., occupational and seasonal) our exercise program should be open to change also. One may find that a change in lifestyle does not necessitate a change in program but one should be open to it.

3 View exercise as a lifetime commitment. You are not training for the Boston Marathon or trying to knock five inches off your waist or add five to your chest. You are working to add to your health for a lifetime or at least as long as you want to be healthy.

4 Avoid setting goals other than the goal to be as healthy as you possibly can be. This is perhaps one of the most difficult things to avoid. Goal setting is largely an

• • • • • • • • • • • • •

outside-in approach. Our society is goal-oriented. Whether it has any value in other areas of life is open to discussion. But it is definitely counterproductive in exercising. You are not trying to reach a preset standard. You are not training with an objective in mind except that of improving your health. Setting goals develops a sense of accomplishment and accomplishment creates an attitude of completing or finishing. Exercise is not something you complete or finish. It is something you plan on doing all your life. Those who set goals must set new goals to keep going. Eventually, they get to setting unrealistic goals which may even be harmful to their health. What is the average person going to do when he or she has reached the goal of running an eight-minute mile? Right, try to run a seven minute mile.

Exercise is the requisite amount of activity to promote adaptation. More than the required amount is no longer exercise but rather, stress. The body has great abilities to adapt in the presence of damaging forces. The educated brain has the ability to mentally overcome the body's warning system. It produces pain killers especially in an activity like running. Pain is often a normal function of the body. It acts as a warning system. When an individual runs, he exercises the body. When he runs too far, the body tells him. Quitting when the body tells you to is wise and sets natural limits to the amount and type of exercise you should be doing for maximum health. Ignoring the message changes exercise to stress. The body can handle great amounts of stress before noticeable damage occurs. The key word is "noticeable." But the health-lowering factor, though not noticeable, is there. Running is a unique exercise because it

•   •   •   •   •   •   •   •   •   •   •   •   •

is also a defense mechanism within the body (part of what is called the "fight or flight" mechanism). Consequently, the body has the ability to overcome the pain and the warnings to allow the individual to continue running. But it is doing harm. I once had a discussion with a friend who claimed that running great distances was not harmful. He had even participated in marathons. Some years later I spoke with him again. He admitted that he was wrong and said the realization came to him after a marathon when he took off his running shoes and his socks were soaked with blood. He had never felt any indication that he was injuring his feet! Goal setting is an educated endeavor. Exercising should be done according to the innate dictates of the body.

5 Listen to your body. If it tells you eight repetitions of a particular exercise are enough, stop. If you feel like walking a block or two during your morning jog, walk it. Don't push yourself. Someone may be saying "*My* exercise is jogging between the refrigerator and the couch in front of the television." Health measures are common sense. Use good judgment and you will come closer to getting the exact amount of exercise necessary for increasing your health.

6 Do exercises you enjoy. If you do not enjoy the exercise, unless you are an extremely disciplined individual, you will probably not keep it up. There is even exercise equipment to be set up in front of the television for the individual with couch potato tendencies. Try different exercises until you hit upon the ones that you enjoy and seem to benefit your body the most.

•   •   •   •   •   •   •   •   •   •   •   •   •

Positive Mental Attitudes

Much has been written and discussed on the subject of mental attitude and its role in health, healing and the treatment of disease. The medical profession is somewhat baffled by the stories and case histories that have come to light. Too often the disease and conditions that are "cured" are not the type that can be written off as psychosomatic. What is undoubtedly happening is that individuals are adding to their health level by changing their mental attitude. That elevated level, under some circumstances, is sufficient to take the individual above the level of disease, signs and symptoms, and they appear to have been cured. This is another example of how people get well from diseases by elevating their health level. While we will discuss getting well from disease, this book is not about using health-raising factors to treat disease but using health-raising factors to maximize the probability of your staying healthy.

Positive mental attitude involves the use of the educated mind as a force for health. The problem with using the educated mind is always the same, it can be used for purposes other than what it was intended. It is easily misused. Blocking out pain in the terminal stages of a disease is a medical treatment not related to health. Like any other medical treatment, it may or may not be helpful depending upon the individual and the situation. For this reason, we must be very careful when using the educated brain to develop positive mental attitudes. Certain principles need to be followed.

1 Any approach to developing a positive mental attitude should come from an above-down inside-out viewpoint.

• • • • • • • • • • • • •

It is important to understand the ADIO world and life viewpoint to make sure that the approach is consistent with it. Drugs and alcohol are an extreme example of how people try to use an outside-in approach to create a positive mental attitude. People use stimulants and relaxants as well as illicit drugs to change their mental attitude. If you need drugs and/or alcohol to get you high, to relax or to give you a positive mental attitude, then either you shouldn't be high or you have an internal cause that needs to be corrected. It is not difficult to see the dangers of this approach. There are, however, other approaches taught in seminars under various names that are just as much outside-in approaches, and probably just as dangerous and just as temporary and addicting as drugs and alcohol. If the approach is not one that enables you to move toward an independent and natural direction, its value is questionable. Approaches that depend upon an individual, a group, a ritual or putting the educated brain in a state of altered consciousness are not consistent with the ADIO philosophy. If you are using your educated mind and you have positive mental attitudes, it makes sense to remain in control of your thinking. An educated mind that is functioning but is divorced from reality, and therefore unable to think in a natural, logical manner, is functioning abnormally. Putting yourself or being put into trances, altered states of consciousness and hypnotic states is not consistent with an inside-out viewpoint.

2 Developing a positive mental attitude should be directed toward removing interferences. Like any other organ of the body, the educated brain functions better without any interference. One such interference might be nerve interference from misaligned bones in the spine. Other interferences may include negative thoughts, guilt, stress and negative emotions, just to name a few. The educated brain needs what other organs need to function: proper rest, exercise and nutrition. It also needs the appropriate input. Good information needs to be placed in it. That is the reason for this book. There is a good deal of garbage in the world, from newspapers and television to our daily contacts. Some of it is unavoidable. But we should try to balance out the bad with good. Read uplifting, positive articles and books, ones that have an ADIO perspective. Limitations of matter may only allow the organ to work at a certain level. That level is established, in part, by the information placed in it. It is like a computer. Some computer programs have limitations. The programming of the disk only allows it to perform certain functions. That is why they keep coming out with new versions. Our educated brain is limited by the quality and quantity of information placed in it. Make sure it is of the highest quality and strive for increasing the quantity. Again, make sure that the information placed in it is filtered through the ADIO world and life viewpoint to keep the garbage out.

3 Your positive mental attitude should almost become natural and automatic. Most educated functions that are done on a regular, repetitive basis become almost automatic, i.e., hitting a baseball, playing the piano or ironing a shirt. If developing and maintaining a positive mental attitude does not become a natural,

• • • • • • • • • • • •

automatic process after a period of time, then there is probably something wrong with your approach and it should be re-evaluated.

This is far from a definitive work on positive mental attitude as a health-raising factor. It is not meant to be. In fact, there are probably volumes that could be written on the subject. This text is not meant to be exhaustive. It is meant to help the reader understand the importance of raising his/her health level; how diet, exercise, rest and a positive mental attitude can contribute to raising the health level, and to give the reader a few principles that can be used in that endeavor.

It should be noted that there is a maximum amount that can be contributed by each of the health-raising factors. Eating twice as much good food as you need will obviously not double your health. Nor will doing more exercise than needed. As we have seen, too much of either of these could be harmful to one's health. Furthermore, no health-raising measure will take the place of another. Exercise is not a substitute for proper eating habits, nor can it make up for poor eating habits. You cannot say, "I'll jog three miles instead of two to make up for the extra helping of chocolate cake." It doesn't work that way. And finally, each measure needs to be done on a regular basis to maximize your health potential. You can't get a good night's sleep all week and then not sleep on the weekend and expect to express your maximum health potential. There may be other health-raising factors which science has yet to discover. There is also a factor that we will be looking at a little later, one that puts all the health-raising measures in a proper perspective.

In the next chapter we will be discussing those factors that drain off our health. They are the ones usually addressed by a disease-treating outside-in philosophy. While it is impossible to eliminate them, common sense measures can keep them to a minimum. In doing that, we can be sure that the major factor in maintaining a high level of health will be what we add to the bucket. In this way, life becomes a positive activity, pro-active in that you are *filling* the bucket, rather than a negative activity, trying to patch up holes and react to the apparent negatives in life.

Let's look at how our health is drained off.

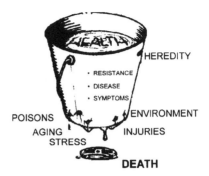

THE
LEAKY BUCKET

Wouldn't it be great if
our bucket would never spring a leak? But then it would also
be great if there were no potholes, no holes in the ozone, and
the kids did not wear holes in the knees of their jeans. Life
and health are full of holes. We should be aware of them and
find out how we are equipped to overcome them. Health
lowering factors are not primary causes of a loss of health
but they should be addressed with a mindset that will keep
them to a minimum. Unfortunately, those in the medical
field have focused almost all their energy, time and money
on addressing these factors. This would not be so bad except
for the mistaken impression they have that by addressing
these factors they can have the greatest impact upon health.
They can have an impact, but it is minimal. Furthermore,
most of that positive effect can be brought about by a little

common sense on the part of ADIO-thinking people rather than by the technological/scientific accomplishments of an outside-in thinking individual in a laboratory, being subsidized by a pharmaceutical industry that has an economic interest in the results. That may sound a little harsh. But overall, more positive effects on disease have been the result of common-sense hygiene measures than medical/drug research. Application of the 2500-year-old Mosaic Law has done more in the battle against disease then all the vaccinations and preventative measures of medicine. Realizing that it is not smart to drink water that has been contaminated or to live among rats has saved more lives than Jenner, Salk, et al.

The other problem with the outside-in approach to tertiary factors is that often the treatment is worse than the disease. You cannot add "too much health" to the bucket. But in trying to plug up the holes you may do more harm than good. In trying to wipe out germs, medical science has created "super germs" resistant to virtually all forms of antibiotic therapy. We will discuss the idea that the treatment is sometimes worse than the problem, where applicable throughout this chapter.

Environment

The environment is a health-lowering factor. If we lived in a perfect environment, it would not be a factor. Sadly, we do not. The environment always challenges our ability to adapt. Environmental effects can be divided into two categories: the natural environment and the unnatural environment.

The Natural Environment

The natural environment is rarely thought of as being dangerous to your health. But the forces of the universe do tend to be destructive to our physical bodies, robbing us of our health. It is not unnatural. It assures that species with a high level of health will survive. It also makes room for new people, animals, and plants and prevents overcrowding of the planet. But the natural environment is not to be feared since we do have the ability to live in the natural environment and adapt those destructive tendencies for our benefit, within certain limitations. If we understand those tendencies, understand that we have limitations and use common sense we can use the natural environment for our benefit without suffering from its destructive potential. It is like an automobile. It is a highly destructive tool of transportation, the most destructive. More people are killed by automobiles than by every other means of transportation combined. However, all things considered, it is the most efficient means of transportation the world has ever seen. If we understand its tendencies toward destruction, understand our limitations (e.g., inability to effectively react at extremely high speeds), and use common sense, we can overcome its destructive tendencies and use it for our benefit.

Sun

The sun is a perfect example in our natural environment. It tends to be destructive to matter. It will rob a living organism of its moisture and damage the human skin. This destructive tendency is not necessarily all bad. The sun's ability to cause water to evaporate is partially responsible for weather patterns. Its destructive characteristic toward organic matter is also a necessary component of decomposition which is important to the chemical cycles of life. What's more, as living organisms we have the ability to use this potentially destructive environmental force for constructive purposes. We use the sun to grow food and also to produce Vitamin D. We, as living organisms, have the ability to adapt to it, producing melanin in the skin (which causes us to tan) to reduce the potential to burn (destroy tissue). But we are limited. Time limits our ability to produce melanin so staying out in the sun too long can cause destruction of the skin cells. Here is where common sense comes into the picture. Limiting the health-reducing effects of the natural environment involves a body that is working properly, producing chemicals to form vitamins and melanin, and common sense. Common sense, as we have already stated, is listening to your body, avoiding extreme temperatures when there are indications that your body is not comfortable in those situations.

Gravity

Gravity is a natural environmental factor. It is a simple example. It can damage and destroy tissues and even cause loss of life (a fall from a tall structure). It can be adapted and used for good. Without gravity we could not even walk down a flight of steps. Common sense will keep us from being injured by it. Avoiding jumping from heights that may cause injury or death is common sense. One would have no reservation about jumping from a one-foot height. But if you have to stop and think about whether to jump from a certain height, that height is probably too great.

Bacteria

Bacteria are a part of our natural environment. They tend to be destructive toward matter. Like the sun, they contribute to the necessary decomposition of organic matter. They can also be used by the organism in a positive way just like the sun and gravity. E. Coli is a bacteria that is found naturally in the digestive tract of human beings. Its very destructive nature is used by the body to help in the breakdown of food for digestion. Common sense is of minimal value in living in a natural environment with bacteria. Perhaps that is because under natural circumstances bacteria cannot be seen or their presence known. They are not visible to our senses so we do not have to use common sense about them. We are not given abilities that we do not need. Therefore common sense is of little value in contrast to the sun and gravity. Common sense says do not stay out too long in the sun or jump off of tall buildings. When it comes to bacteria in a natural environment, we do not need to use common sense. In a perfect natural environment, bacteria will not cause problems. However, our environment is not always perfect. For example, bacteria may grow in food that has spoiled. This, then, becomes part of the unnatural environment.

In summary, the natural environment is in many ways a threat to our health level. However, we have been given the necessary tools to reduce its potential harm to us and live comfortably within it. The unnatural environment is an altogether different matter.

• • • • • • • • • • • • •

The Unnatural Environment

Man has created many situations in which the environment has been made unnatural. It is enough of a challenge to the organism to adapt to the natural environment without creating unnatural situations. But that is exactly what we have done. The air has been polluted by chemicals, exhaust, cigarette smoke and dozens of other pollutants. We have created situations in which germs, which are part of the natural environment, have become part of an unnatural environment, existing in great numbers or reproducing in dangerous and resistive forms. As a result of making micro-oganisms, a non-threatening part of our natural environment, part of our unnatural environment, we can no longer depend on common sense but must develop some elaborate procedures and laws to use our educated brain wisely in compensating for this unnatural environment. These include everything from the Mosaic Law concerning hygiende to state laws requiring food handling employees to wash their hands after a visit to the lavatory. Governmental municipalities have altered our water supply, making it unnatural. Practical solutions to these problems will be discussed under the topic of hygiene but at this point it is enough to know that they do lower our health.

Age

Age is a health-lowering factor, although probably not as great a factor as people are led to believe. We tend to blame our inability to do the things that we once did on our age. That inability is due more to a lowering of the health level rather than age alone. There are many people who remain very active at 60, 70, 80 and even 90 years of age.

•   •   •   •   •   •   •   •   •   •   •   •

They are doing so because they have been careful not to do things to lower their health level and instead, consistently add to their health level. Some of these people are even engaged in activities that they could not do at an earlier age. Wouldn't it be great to have more energy and stamina at age 80 than at age 45? It can be done. At a certain point in their life they decided to add to their health level by doing those things necessary to be healthy. They have improved their eating habits, taken up exercise. The age factor, while still there, has minimal effect upon them. Isn't it interesting that those individuals who choose the disease-treatment route may occasionally get back to functioning and feeling like they did before they got the disease but they almost never reach a level of performance and health that they had when they were a teenager or young adult. People who have a gall bladder removed may say they feel better than they did with gall stones but they rarely say they feel better than they did at age eighteen. People adding to their health level will tell you they feel as good or better than they did fifty years ago.

We must be careful not to blame sickness and disease on age. Age is a tertiary factor. The failure to add to your health level as you get older is the more important factor. It has been suggested by some authorities for example that beginning to exercise even in later years, will increase the health level.

It does appear that there is a relationship between age and an increasing depletion of health as the years go by. The human body is not able to live forever so it seems that age must be an increasing factor in health depletion. But we must be careful not to make more of this factor or any tertiary factor than we should. The human body is capable of living a great deal longer than the average life span and probably greater than even the longest living individuals.

Stress

Stress is another health-lowering factor. Much is made of stress as a factor in disease. Perhaps it is overrated. Like other tertiary factors its influence on an individual's health level will be determined by other factors. Stress appears to have no effect on some people while others appear to crack under the slightest bit of pressure. This is a perfect example of why tertiary factors should not be of prime concern with regard to an individual's health. It is also an example of why tertiary factors are best taken care of by the individual himself or herself. Each person is in the best position to realize what causes them stress and how to handle it. In other words, you are in the best position to keep this hole in the bucket to a minimum. Perhaps stress is getting so much attention today because people who subject themselves to stress tend to neglect health-raising measures and as a result lower their health level far enough to manifest a disease. Business and professional people who are in great stress occupations often do not take the time or make the time to exercise. Their diets are often poor and they may not be getting the proper amount of rest on a regular basis. There are many high profile, highly stressed individuals who are as dedicated to maintaining their health level and reducing the health-lowering factors as they are to their business or profession. These are successful, healthy, happy, productive people. To them, health has become a priority. As a

•   •   •   •   •   •   •   •   •   •   •   •

health-raising factor, a good mental attitude is very important in handling adversity · and not allowing it to become stress.

Poisons

This category of health-lowering factors includes substances that we ingest, inhale and inject into our bodies. Some are part of the environment mentioned earlier, some are of our own choosing. They harm the tissues and lower the health level of the individual. A logical above-down inside-out approach to handling this problem will be discussed in the section on hygiene.

Heredity

This category is unique. It is a continual or ongoing health-lowering factor but one which we have little control over. It has become the catch-all of the medical profession because it fits into their disease model (as do all health-lowering factors) as a cause of ill health. It gets them off the hook in failing to successfully wage war against disease. People recognize heredity as a foe, as they do a bacteria or virus. But while heredity absolves the medical profession of the responsibility for failure to successfully overcome disease, it also absolves the patient of responsibility. They can say that it is not their fault, it is their parents' or better yet, their grandparents' fault. This way they can blame it on someone else. Of course, if they are around, your grandparents could blame your "heredity problems" on *their* grandparents.

The story is told of B.J. Palmer attending a medical lecture entitled "No spit, no consumption." Palmer was perhaps the most outstanding developer of the

• • • • • • • • • • • •

above-down-inside-out philosophy as it relates to health. While the story is not really one of heredity but environment, it demonstrates the foolishness of blaming disease on our ancestors. The talk was given in the early part of the century. The medical doctor was presenting the outside-in theory that spitting on the sidewalk caused consumption (an old term for tuberculosis). In fact, until very recently, subways in many large cities had signs saying "no spitting" attesting to the belief. When it came time for questions, B.J. raised his hand and asked where the person who spit got consumption. The answer was that somebody before him spit to give it to him. B.J., with a twinkle in his eye, said to the physician, "well I guess Adam then is responsible for all the consumption in the world." The M.D. thought for a minute then smiled and agreed. To which B.J. replied, "But there was nobody around to spit before Adam!"

If you try to find the logic in the outside-in theory of disease you invariably run into a brick wall. It just does not make sense. While heredity is a factor, it is only an influencing factor. To blame it for disease is to ignore primary and secondary causes. Paying attention to the primary and secondary causes are the responsibility of the individual. Tertiary causes are unavoidable under normal circumstances. Heredity, as a factor, is more like a hole at the top of the bucket setting the limit to which an individual's health level can rise. Even though it is a health-lowering factor its nature (limiting the level) is important. It rarely prevents an individual from experiencing a full and productive life.

The human body is a fantastic organism with tremendous power and ability to overcome and compensate for handicaps. Genetics will prevent us from rising above a certain level. But if we concentrate on health-raising measures we can rise to a level that will enable us to lead a full and productive life, regardless of our so-called genetic handicaps. The worst thing an individual can do is to give up and resign himself to a life less than *his* fullest. Heredity is only a predisposition. It can be overcome. There are thousands of people with all kinds of so-called hereditary diseases in their family history who never get the diseases. They concentrate on keeping their health level high. Heredity is a primary cause in reaching the maximum health level but merely a tertiary factor in disease. This is an important concept to understand and accept. So many diseases and problems are being blamed on the heredity factor. Diseases like diabetes, heart problems and cancer are being blamed on heredity. There was a story in the paper not too long ago about a young woman who had a double radical mastectomy. She was perfectly healthy but there was a history of breast cancer in her family. This kind of thinking demonstrates the harm that can be done by an overemphasis upon heredity as a cause of disease. A great deal is being written now concerning obesity being an heredity problem. This outside-in thinking, to blame disease (if it is a disease) on heredity may have the detrimental effect of causing thousands of people to say, "what's the use, why should I bother to exercise or be careful in my eating habits if I am condemned by my genes to obesity." The outside-in approach has inherent dangers to it.

•   •   •   •   •   •   •   •   •   •   •   •

Hygiene

When we think of the subject of hygiene, we are invariably drawn back to high school health class and those embarrassing talks on personal hygiene. While that is an important aspect of hygiene, it is only a very minor part. Hygiene has been defined as "the restoration of natural and healthful environmental conditions which have been made abnormal by the necessities of civilized life." We cannot live as animals in the wild, ignoring the rules of society and the rights of our fellow man. The very number of people living together in relatively small areas necessitates compromise. However, making these concessions does not mean we must accept a life of less than ideal health. Civilization imposes many interferences, challenges and difficulties upon adaptation. By understanding the philosophy of ADIO health care, understanding the role of the innate intelligence of the body in adapting to the environment and, most important, understanding the role of the educated intelligence, we can better remove the interferences and meet the challenges.

Above-down philosophy is largely common sense based upon logical, deductive reasoning. In applying it to the subject of hygiene, we are merely using logical principles. We understand that human beings living close together have created environmental problems in the area of drinking water, for example.

Three hundred years ago, in the undeveloped parts of this country, an individual could go down to the river or a stream and scoop out a drink of clear, pure water. Three hundred years ago you could not do that in Europe. People had polluted the rivers and streams. The increase in population has created the same situation in this country where drinking from rivers and streams and even many wells is currently unsafe. However, governmental municipalities' approach to the problem is characterized by their outside-in, disease-oriented viewpoint, rather than a health viewpoint. They have demonstrated to their satisfaction that water carries micro-organisms that may cause diseases such as typhoid and hepatitis. As a treatment they dump strong chemicals into the water to destroy the organisms. But these chemicals are also harmful to health, even though it has not been scientifically and "conclusively" proven that these chemicals cause disease from an outside-in viewpoint. Because it has not been proven, they are continually used. But they are poisons and can certainly influence our level of health. Disease is the result or perception of a lack of health at a particular level. How can we make this claim that they decrease our health without scientific proof? We use a scientific law. There is a principle that says that what is true at a noticeable level is also true on the unnoticeable level. A brick placed in a bucket of water will raise the level of the water in proportion to the mass of the brick. It is measurable (noticeable). A brick placed in Lake Michigan will also raise the level of the Lake even though it will not be noticed. Applying that principle to our discussion of water, if I drink a glass full of liquid chlorine that I would usually dump in my swimming pool, I would become deathly ill. Common sense and logic say, then, that small amounts of chlorine in water will lower the health level of my body if only imperceptably. It may have never made anyone sick, but every time you drink a glass of chlorinated water, you open

•   •   •   •   •   •   •   •   •   •   •   •   •

a small hole in your bucket. Until research proves that chlorinated water causes disease, those that hold an outside-in viewpoint, will not see its danger. Unfortunately, no one is very likely researching that possibility. But more important, our concern should be not that it is causing a disease but that it is contributing to the decline of an individual's health, and that together, with other factors, will reduce the level to the point that the signs and symptoms of some disease will become apparent.

Common sense says that we should not drink water contaminated with micro-organisms. But it also says that we should not drink water contaminated with poisonous chemicals. We need to find a way of eliminating the former without subjecting our bodies to the latter. Sadly, there are a number of factors that come into play in this situation. Cleaning up the water without poisonous chemicals may be more expensive and more time consuming. Often these chemicals are the by-products of industry. What would ordinarily be toxic waste and cost an industry great sums of money to dispose of is seen as having some benefit to us, and it is dumped in our water. The human body is probably the worst toxic dump site in the country. Above-down hygiene is concerned with bringing the water back to a healthy state, not ridding it of disease. The thrust of this book is bringing the body back to a healthy state (and keeping it there), not ridding it of disease. This is just an extension of that thinking.

Another example of outside-in thinking regarding water is the addition of a strong chemical, fluoride, in an effort to prevent a disease - dental cavities. My community has had fluoride in its drinking water for over forty years. No one has ever studied the effect it has upon people's health. This is not naturally occurring fluoride. Is it damaging other tissues, perhaps kidney tissue. It's easier to replace teeth than kidneys. I wonder too, why do some kids in my community still have bad teeth? Don't they drink the water? Why are there still dentists in business after all these years? We need some legitimate and impartial studies. Of course, you really do not have to study it. Common sense says that if you put a strong chemical in the water, you must decrease the health potential of those drinking it. The entire issue of pure drinking water needs a tremendous amount of thought. However, until those making the decisions do so from an above-down, inside-out perspective, how we treat our water will continue to demonstrate the disease-treating, outside-in thinking. Considering that water is the most important commodity to the life and well-being of man, our attitudes must change.

Ideally, we should be working toward allowing the innate intelligence of the body to adapt to the environment in a better manner by removing any and all interferences to it. While the innate wisdom is a fantastic principle, it is limited by the matter of the body. We cannot adapt to strong poisons put in our food, for example. So we have an educated brain to tell us not to place poisons in our food. ADIO hygiene is the proper use of the educated brain.

Civilization has created tremendous problems, greater than the innate wisdom can handle due to limitations of time and matter. Common sense hygiene can resolve many of these problems. The approach is two-fold. First, we must address hygiene from a personal standpoint. We must avoid putting poisonous substances in our body with the food we eat, the water we drink and the air we breathe. Second, and this is the more difficult part, we must work toward changing the environment back to a more natural, less harmful state. However, we must also be conscious of the demands of society. For example, we could outlaw automobiles and improve the air immensely. But the quality of life would be decreased by preventing us the freedom and the mobility that the automobile gives us. As individuals, we can work toward making our own personal environment more healthful, while society as a whole works on the general environment.

Until clear-thinking people are able to recognize the need for pure, chemical-free water and develop the technology to provide it, we must find other sources if we want to drink pure water. You may decide to use bottled spring water that comes from a reputable company with quality assurance or personal water-purifying systems. I am not recommending or advising one or the other. As already mentioned, the intent of this book is for you, the individual, to take responsibility and make your own decisions about every aspect of your health.

Food

With regard to food, we must recognize that any substance that the body cannot use for metabolism has the potential to reduce the health of the individual and should be avoided. It is not necessary to find statistics, do studies and research. If in great amounts, it is a poison and has no nutritional value, then in small amounts it is also a poison. We do not know whether the body can get rid of it, whether it can rid itself of all of it or how much damage is being done in the process. Poisons should be avoided. But most of all, we must change the thinking that says that a chemical that is foreign to the body can benefit it. This includes chemicals on our fruits and vegetables, additives and preservatives and any other chemicals placed in the food. Every time you take a food additive into your body, you may be springing a leak. The body may be able to repair these leaks up to a point, but the health level is depleted.

Drugs

The amount of drugs, both prescription and over-the-counter, that are pumped into the body in pursuit of health is unbelievable. While they have saved lives and may even allow people to function in a more productive manner (or in the case of psychotropic drugs be less of a menace to society) none of them have ever raised the level of health in an individual in the sense of health that we are discussing in this book. Sometimes they may be needed to treat disease but the mindset must be that any drug is a poison to the body and should be avoided as much as possible. Most other aspects of hygiene from an above-down perspective are primarily common sense.

Trauma

Trauma and injury need to be understood in light of this health/entity and disease/non-entity concept. Trauma treatment is a legitimate part of the practice of medicine. Injuries or traumas may well require emergency attention.

Trauma is a health-lowering experience. It is like one of the holes in the bucket. The size of the hole, of course, will determine the degree of health loss. A small hole, such as a

• • • • • • • • • • • • •

cut finger, will cause an imperceptible loss of health. A severe trauma could be like the entire bottom of the bucket giving way and causing an instantaneous loss of all health. This would occur in a fatal injury. One of the interesting aspects of trauma is that a body experiencing a high level of health has the ability to heal itself of most traumas, providing common-sense measures are applied. Keeping a cut clean and free of dirt, immobilizing a fracture and a severe sprain are just common-sense measures. If applied, the loss of health is minimal and healing occurs with no complications. Conversely, an individual with a low level of health may succumb to what, in most circumstances, may be a minor trauma. A relatively few years ago, a not uncommon "cause" of death among older people was a fractured hip from a fall. "Complications" is a simple way of saying that the health level of the individual was so low that an injury, which under ordinary circumstances would not cause a problem, caused the person's death.

The concept of complications is also applicable to diseases and surgery. People with lowered resistance (low health level), die from seemingly minor diseases. The same applies to surgical procedures. Many a surgery has been successful but the patient died due to complications. Surgical procedures, whether necessary or not, are a trauma to the body and must be viewed as such. If medicine would begin to try to measure health levels and work toward raising those levels in patients needing surgery, perhaps they could reduce the incidence of death due to surgical complications. Of course, if medicine would begin measures to raise the health level, the need for surgical procedures would surely decrease.

The difference between the above-down and the outside-in approaches really rests in how each group views the holes in the bucket and their importance relative to the health level. The ADIO viewpoint is to concentrate on adding to the bucket and using common sense measures to keep the holes to a minimum. The OIBU approach is to focus almost solely on the holes and trying to patch them, usually temporarily. Often in doing this, they end up creating more holes than they reduce.

8
DOES IT
REALLY MATTER
HOW YOU FEEL?

While symptoms may or may not
require treatment, from an above-down perspective, they are
a fact of life and health. Their existence is real and an
understanding of their role in health is necessary. Further,
anyone desiring a life based upon health-enhancing measures and desiring to reduce disease treatment to a minimum,
should understand the part symptoms play in health, disease
and well-being.

There are three categories of symptoms from a
above-down standpoint. They are adaptive symptoms, innate
expression symptoms and limitation symptoms. An understanding of these categories will enable anyone to see why
the person experiencing the symptoms is often the best
person to treat the symptoms or determine whether they
should be treated.

It should be noted that the patient as well as probably any doctor often cannot tell which category a symptom is in, making it even more difficult to determine how it is impacting the patient's health. With that in mind, let us explore these categories of symptoms.

A Definition

A symptom has been described as an indication that the body is reaching the outer limits of its adaptive ability (the ability to live in and handle the environment). That is a fairly good working definition. Clearly, when the body passes the outer limits of its adaptive ability, all symptoms cease. Death is the lack of adaptation and there are no symptoms. That is a pretty obvious conclusion. Not so clear and perhaps open to argument is the assumption that if the body is adapting perfectly, it should never have any symptoms. Such a notion is based upon the mistaken assumption that all symptoms are bad and if the body were completely well (if a body can be completely well), it would not express any symptoms. It is also based upon the assumption that we live in a perfect environment. Symptoms arise from the inability of the body to adapt to external invasive forces (factors such as bacteria, poisons and trauma). Engaging in every possible health-raising measure guarantees nothing more than the fact that the individual will be better able to adapt, not necessarily perfectly, just better. But there are still limitations of matter

> A symptom indicates that the body is reaching the outer limits of its adaptive ability

• • • • • • • • • • • • •

that come into play. Under normal circumstances the body can adapt to external invasive forces and symptoms will not occur. Unfortunately, we do not live under normal circumstances.

The world is an imperfect place, consequently we are subjected to abnormal external invasive forces and abnormal circumstances. Accidents happen. Falling down a flight of steps is not a normal circumstance. When our bodies are unable to adapt to these forces, symptoms occur. Having an automobile strike your car from behind is an example of an imperfect world, with imperfect drivers! Stepping off a curb is a normal part of every day life. It should cause no symptoms because the body is able to adapt under usual circumstances. Jumping out of a three-story window will move the body toward the outer limits of adaptability and cause symptoms (the pain of legs breaking, or more likely, death!). Perhaps a more realistic example or two may help.

The body was designed to be resistant to microorganisms in a natural and normal amount. Regularly practicing health-raising measures will help enable the body to live in this environment with these viruses and never show symptoms. There are viruses and bacteria constantly in the air, and even in our respiratory tract. That is a perfectly normal part of the environment in which we function and adapt. But having someone sneeze or cough in your face and subject your respiratory tract to billions more viruses is not normal or natural. That may be more than even a strong, healthy body can handle (limitations of matter), in which case symptoms will appear. These symptoms, although unpleasant, are the innate intelligence trying to make the

●　●　●　●　●　●　●　●　●　●　●　●

body normal in an abnormal environment. That process is called adaptation.

Another example, involves the ever-present bacteria in the food that we eat. That is normal and natural. However, if the food is prepared without concern for hygiene, an abnormal amount of bacteria could get in the food, causing symptoms following ingestion. Symptoms may occur either because of an abnormal exposure to viruses, bacteria, toxin, poisons, etc. or because the body may be weakened and cannot adapt to normal amounts in the environment. Of course, other factors could also weaken the individual, such as a genetic defect. The "boy in the bubble" is an example of an immune system that cannot even handle normal exposure to micro-organisms. If a perfect body were adapting perfectly to a perfect environment, it would never have symptoms. But we do not have a perfect body and we definitely do not have a perfect environment. Some of that imperfection is, of course, our own fault (pollution, drugs, food additives, etc.).

With that introduction, let's look at the three types of symptoms.

Adaptive Symptoms

Symptoms, as described above, result from adaptation occurring in the body. They may be results of the body adapting to a normal environment but with a lowered ability to adapt, or the body adapting to an abnormal environment, i.e., someone coughing into your face. These symptoms are always a result of the body adapting. If symptoms are occurring in a body that is working at its highest possible level, then they are good. It means the body is successfully fighting something foreign. It is possible that an individual could find himself in a situation or an environment in which the external invasive forces are greater than they should be. That's bad! In other words, when someone looks like they are going to cough in your face, get out of the way! So adaptive symptoms are good, even though they may feel bad. Of course, even if the body is working at its highest possible level, it may still be unable to effectively adapt to external forces. Fever, which we have already discussed in Chapter 5, is an adaptive mechanism that the body uses whether working at its peak or not. When the body is trying to fight off micro-organisms, whether in "normal" amounts in a body with a lowered-health level or in greater than normal amounts (someone's coughing again!), it will elevate the body's temperature to accomplish all that is necessary to enable the body to adapt. We have discussed earlier the research at the University of Michigan, demonstrating how antibody production, interferon production, and a number of other activities that fight infection occur with increased efficiency at higher temperatures.

Vomiting and diarrhea are two other symptoms, also discussed earlier, that can, at times, be adaptive symptoms - signs of a healthy body. The body may be fighting off an invasion of a micro-organism and needs all its strength to do so. The digestion of food takes a good deal of energy and much of the body's attention. We all know that a person may drown if swimming after a meal because the blood rushes to the digestive tract and is insufficient for the large leg muscles, resulting in cramps and the inability to stay afloat.

●　　●　　●　　●　　●　　●　　●　　●　　●　　●　　●　　●

Similarly, the body, not wanting food during an adaptive process, may innately empty the stomach's contents. This is a perfectly normal result of the body adapting. In the same way, getting rid of a poison or otherwise noxious agent that has been ingested in abnormally large quantities may cause the body to flush substances out of the system resulting in diarrhea. These are examples of symptoms which are normal adaptive mechanisms of the body. If these were the only symptoms that ever occurred, we would be correct in maintaining that symptoms were good.   But there are other symptoms which are of a different type. It should be noted that often the same symptoms can occur in more than one category.

Innate Expression Symptoms

This type of symptom occurs when the innate intelligence of the body communicates that limitations of the body are being reached (getting back to our original definition) and there is something the educated intelligence can do to enable us to better adapt. To quickly review the function of the educated brain, it is to enable us to adapt to our external environment. We lack fur coats to keep us warm, so we have an educated brain to build a fire. No animal has the educated ability to create fire. Often when the innate intelligence is aware that the outer limits of adaptation are being approached, it will stimulate the educated brain into action. Sometimes this message is perceived as a symptom.

The most common symptom in this category is pain. If you are sitting out in the hot sun on a summer afternoon and the sun begins to have destructive effects upon the body, the innate intelligence will communicate that fact to the educated brain in no uncertain terms. Instinctively, (innately) animals will avoid external invasive factors when they begin to create a threat to their well-being. An animal will seek shade on a hot day, even avoiding the hunt for food. But we are anxious for a "healthy" tan so we sit out in the broiling sun. We think it looks healthy and beautiful. Two hundred years ago women powdered their faces to look pale. That was considered beautiful. The innate intelligence does not care about beauty, it only cares about adaptation. So, the innate intelligence of the body will begin adaptive measures which we are not even aware of as we lay on a blanket at the shore expanding our mind on a collection of Calvin and Hobbes comic strips or some other intellectual endeavor. Melanin is being formed in the skin to prevent tissue damage as a result of burning. Perspiration is taking place to attempt to cool the skin. Blood is being rushed to the areas to help the cooling process. However, the innate intelligence is limited by time and matter. It cannot produce melanin fast enough

and the sweat glands cannot produce sufficient fluids without damaging the organism. So the innate intelligence will communicate to our educated brain through pain and in this example, thirst, the need to educatedly do something to adapt us to our external environment. If we use our educated brain properly, we get out of the sun and drink some fluids. Some may use the educated brain improperly, by ignoring the stinging skin and drinking alcohol. Not that alcohol isn't a fluid, it just promotes the dehydration process.

There are many examples in which the educated brain can be a useful organ to help us adapt when we are reaching the outer limits of our adaptive ability. That is why we have an educated brain. If used in the right way, at the right time, for the right reason, it is a valuable tool. If used incorrectly, it can be life threatening. A loose nail in your shoe that is protruding into your foot will cause pain so that you can remove it. Being in an environment that is irritating to the tissues of the body or is a threat to adaptation will cause the innate intelligence to communicate to the brain to leave that location. Harmful fumes in a closed room are a threat. The brain is stimulated to recognize them as a threat to the body's well-being. The innate intelligence of the body uses every mechanism at its disposal to adapt the organism to its environment. It is perfectly logical that the innate intelligence would use the educated brain also. Often, the only way we are consciously aware of a situation occurring in our body that necessitates educated activity to adapt us, is by the presence of innate expression symptoms or signals from the innate intelligence of the body.

Limitation Symptoms

This category of symptoms consists of ones that occur as a result of limitations of matter, which in turn allow a breakdown to occur in the body's system. These symptoms would include those associated with terminal diseases when the entire system appears to be failing. Limitations symptoms may be chronic. They may also be associated with major degeneration or damage on a limited level. Pain associated with arthritis and other chronic disorders would be in this category. In this situation, the body is breaking down. Damage is occurring to the tissues. The mechanism that normally warns a person of tissue damage, as from a trauma, is set into motion. But the body has no ability or limited ability to heal the tissue, or to shut off the alarm system. Sometimes the body can produce chemicals to overcome the alarm, either permanently or temporarily. This is one reason why those that suffer with arthritis, for example, are not in pain all the time or terminally-ill patients sometimes have periods of relief without medication. But even the body's ability to produce its own pain killers is severely limited in this category.

Symptoms are not the focus

We see then, that there are different categories and causes for symptoms in the human body. You may be experiencing the same symptoms as a friend of yours and yet, they may have different causes. Pain, for example, can occur in all categories. The symptom may also move from one category to another in the same person, especially as the body reaches the outermost limits of its adaptive ability. The pain of a warning may eventually be the pain of a terminally-ill person. Because of the inability to know the reason for symptoms, a true health care professional should not place emphasis upon them, either in treating them or determining what their significance is to an individual's health. That is perhaps the most important point relative to a discussion on health. Symptoms are simply not an indicator of health or necessarily an indicator that the body is reaching its adaptive limits. We have all heard the stories of people who were totally without symptoms, appeared healthy, and died suddenly. We have had plenty of graphic and tragic examples of this in the last few years. Many HIV-positive people are totally without symptoms, yet they have a terminal disease. Symptoms are not a good indication of our state of health. They are not even a good indicator of disease; although they are the primary way the physician determines a disease. Disease should not be the primary focus in a *health* care system.

However, while disease is an absence of health, it is a very real part of a person's life and anyone interested in their health should understand certain basic facts about disease. The first concept to understand relates to the causes of disease.

9

WHAT
CAUSES DISEASE?

Years ago, the medical field attempted
to blame all disease on a single cause. In fact, throughout
early history and the so-called Dark Ages all diseases were
thought to have a single cause. Whether it was evil spirits,
bad blood, or the night air changed with the culture. As
science became more advanced, it became apparent that this
concept was not true. Medical science then began to place
the cause of individual diseases on individual factors. So that
instead of blaming demons for all disease, each individual
disease had a specific, individual cause. The invention of the
microscope and the discovery of micro-organisms merely
perpetuated that thinking. Any time a person had a certain
group of symptoms (a disease) and a specific micro-
organism could be found in great numbers under the
microscope, the conclusion would be, the micro-organism

caused the disease. As a result, it was thought that strep-tococcus caused strept throat, pneumococcus caused pneumonia, mycobacterium leprae caused leprosy and so on. The problem is that these organisms can often be found in perfectly healthy people.

Above-down thinking suggests there are numerous factors or causes involved in every disease. For example, it would be foolish to claim that viruses or bacteria were not factors in a number of diseases. Some who speak against this above-down thinking attack us by saying we do not believe in germs or the germ theory. It is not a matter of belief. You can see them under a microscope. But seeing them and considering them *the cause* are two alto-gether different concepts. As we understand the entire concept of the cause of disease, we shall see that there are so many factors or "causes" that it becomes absurd to attempt to establish a cause-effect relationship. Consider the following scenario: Uncle Charlie comes to visit the family and while there plays with each of the five children. Unfortunately, he has a cold and when he leaves, four of the five children are also showing signs and symptoms of a cold. Of these four, one is sick for three days, one for a week, one two weeks and the other ends up with pneumonia. The virus was a factor but if it was the only factor, all five should have gotten his cold and all five should have had it for the same length of time. This simple illustration proves there must be other factors.

> Above-down thinking suggests there are numerous factors or causes involved in every disease

•   •   •   •   •   •   •   •   •   •   •   •   •

Especially since one developed pneumonia. The virus associated with the common cold and the one associated with pneumonia are different!

Lack of resistance is a factor or a cause. Failing to engage in health-raising measures may be a factor. For this reason, above-down thinking people have concluded that there are multiple causes for every disease. These factors can be divided into three major categories which may induce those relating to disease to place a different degree of importance on different factors. Categorizing them enables us to better understand their importance and therefore, how to address our attention to them, just as everyone, including those in the health field, should. If one factor is more important than another, perhaps our attention should be focused primarily on the more important one. If some causes predispose toward disease while others merely influence the process, perhaps we should address the predisposing factors.

Recently the Center for Disease Control (CDC) released figures indicating that the incidence of cancer deaths attributed to smoking has decreased. Of course, the CDC is an outside-in-thinking governmental agency. The question that this raised in my mind is, "What happens to the 50,000 or so smokers who are not dying of lung cancer? Do they live forever? Do they all die in auto- mobile accidents? Are they dying of another form of cancer? If we are reducing lung cancer but other forms of cancer like colon, breast and skin are increasing in proportion, shouldn't our research be in another direction? Our research only reflects our mindset, which

•   •   •   •   •   •   •   •   •   •   •   •   •

says that cigarette smoking is the cause of cancer. Don't misunderstand, cigarette smoking is certainly not good for one's health. It is detrimental to one's health. The air you breathe is an environmental hole in your bucket and there is nothing worse than inhaling bad air on purpose. But to blame cancer on smoking, to the point of ignoring some other, perhaps more important factors, gets us nowhere. If there are predisposing factors to cancer, then it does not matter whether you smoke or not. If you do not get lung cancer, you may get colon or liver or breast cancer. Blaming cancer on smoking blinds us to other factors. We must look at all possible causes and factors. There obviously are other factors. The very fact that some people smoke for seventy years and never get lung cancer while others die from the disease never having smoked a cigarette in their life proves this.

In our discussion we will present three categories of factors which cause disease: primary, secondary and tertiary. For disease to occur there must be at least a primary and a secondary factor. The most common diseases (the majority) also require a tertiary factor, although these diseases are the least fatal because they respond to medical treatment or any treatment better. To say that any category is more important than another in the *treatment of disease* is presumptuous. However, as we understand the three categories and their relationship to disease, it will become apparent why some professions have chosen to direct their attention to a primary factor only. For while no category is more

> There are three categories of factors which causes disease: primary, secondary, and tertiary

important in the *treatment of disease*, when it comes to *health maintenance*, which is our main concern in the writing of this book, certain categories do appear to have more importance than others. For this reason we have chosen to describe these three categories as primary factors, secondary factors and tertiary factors.

Primary Factors

Primary factors are limitations of the body. Examples of these factors include genetic defects, congenital conditions, and the inability of the innate intelligence of the body to be expressed because of interference in its methods of expression, particularly the nervous system.

Their Cause is Outside Your Control

The cause of primary factors in disease is outside the control of the individual. Whenever you look at cause and effect, you eventually get back to a cause that you, under normal circumstances, have no control over. It is true that we all make choices that affect our lives and are responsible for those choices. In this category, however, if the individual is responsible for causing the primary factor, it occurs out of ignorance. One may choose to drive down a certain street where he has an accident that causes the loss of a spleen (causing limitations of matter in the body). Of course, he did not drive down that street with the intention of having that accident. One may decide to take up skiing knowing full well he will take a few spills but not intending to permanently damage himself. Genetic weaknesses are also limitations of the body which the individual definitely has no control over. They come from the parents. A primary cause then is one over which, under usual circumstances, the individual has no control.

They Do Not Show Themselves as Disease

Primary factors do not show themselves as diseases. They alone are not a disease. Secondary and/or tertiary factors must be present before disease occurs. This is why the medical profession has directed its attention toward tertiary factors. While a primary factor alone does not manifest disease, when the tertiary factor is present, disease will occur. Medical science incorrectly concludes that the tertiary factor is the cause. It is the old "straw that broke the camel's back" principle. The field of medicine addresses the last straw rather than the first million. Medical science deals primarily with causes that can be demonstrated through our senses. Bacteria and viruses can be seen under a microscope. By analogy, we may not know we have forgotten to empty our garbage pail if our sense of smell is not affected. When we see the flies gathering, we know we have forgotten, but we do not blame the *flies* for the garbage or the smell. The medical doctor does not use such reasoning. We may have a sick body due to primary and secondary factors, a body lacking health, but when the tertiary factor (the bacteria), arrives, the medical doctor blames the disease on them. Remember, primary factors do not show themselves as disease.

They Decrease Your Potential

Primary factors cause the body to function at a lower level than it should. They do not manifest themselves as disease but they do decrease the potential of an individual to reach what the human organism is intended to be. Further,

•   •   •   •   •   •   •   •   •   •   •   •

they create a fixed level of health in the person, above which they are never able to rise. No matter what else is done for that person, he/she can never reach beyond the level established by the primary factor(s). Secondary and tertiary factors may further reduce that level but eliminating those factors cannot raise health above the level established by the primary factor. An individual with an organ missing can never be as healthy as he/she would be with it. For example, a physician may remove a diseased appendix. The patient is less sick (his symptoms are gone), but he is not healthier. A person with an organ missing is not healthier than a person with an organ not working properly. Removing an organ is a limitation of matter. A primary cause always has the same effect in every person every time. It causes the body to function less than it should.

They Need Another Person to Correct Them

Primary factors necessitate another person to correct them. The primary cause is out of the control of the individual. Someone or something else is necessary to correct it, if indeed it can be corrected. Many limitations of the body cannot be corrected. An organ transplant or an artificial limb would be measures that could be taken for severe limitations of the body. If it is a genetic defect, nothing can be done.

Secondary Factors

Secondary factors include poor diet, lack of exercise and rest, and poor mental attitude. They are the faucets in our bucket analogy.

Again, it should be emphasized that just because they are secondary, does not mean that they are not important. It is just that they have different characteristics.

They Can Be Controlled by the Individual

Secondary factors can be controlled by the individual. We control the opening or the closing of the faucet. In fact, the correction of these factors is best addressed by the individual himself or herself. The determination of a proper diet and the amount of exercise and rest needed should be determined by the person using their educated intelligence in an appropriate manner while attempting to follow the dictates of the innate intelligence of the body.

They Depend on Primary Factors

Secondary factors depend upon the presence of a primary factor to cause disease. By themselves they cannot cause disease. They necessitate the primary factor being present before a disease is manifested. Some people never exercise and never get a disease associated with lack of exercise. However, they will never reach their maximum health potential. A secondary factor is manifested differently in every person. A primary factor affects everyone the same. Some people will become ill if they only get five hours of sleep a night, while others may remain perfectly healthy. It depends upon their genetic makeup, (limitations of the body's matter) and the ability of their body to maximize the rest they get (integrity of the nervous system). Even a disease like scurvy which is caused by secondary factors (a lack of vitamin C) necessitates a primary factor. It was first discovered in sailors on sailing ships who went for months at sea with no source of vitamin C, the vitamin found in foods such as citrus fruits. The body apparently does not store vitamin C. However, different sailors would show the

•   •   •   •   •   •   •   •   •   •   •   •

symptoms of scurvy at different times and some never got the disease, indicating that a certain health level, established in part by the primary factors, was necessary for the disease to be manifested. A secondary factor is specific for the individual and necessitates a primary factor to cause disease.

They Can Be Directly or Indirectly Related to Disease

Secondary factors can be directly related to disease, or they can predispose you to a tertiary factor. For example, nutritional insufficiency, a secondary factor, can result in disease, in the presence of a primary factor. But that secondary factor can also contribute to lowered resistance, which in the presence of tertiary factors can result in disease.

Tertiary or third ranking factors

Tertiary factors include stress, environment, germs, and pollution.

Tertiary factors occur very close to if not at the same time the disease is able to be recognized. They are so far removed from being a cause that it almost seems foolish to describe them as a "cause." However, they have some characteristics worth noting.

They Depend on Primary and Secondary Factors

Tertiary factors only "cause" disease in the presence of primary and secondary factors. An individual must have a body working at less than its potential for tertiary factors to result in disease. Not only must there be a primary factor but there must often be a secondary factor as well. Lowered resistance in part due to insufficient diet, exercise and rest creates a situation in which ordinarily acceptable levels of external forces, such as micro-organisms, stress, pollution, etc. become important factors.

They Can Determine the Nature of Disease

Tertiary factors will often determine the nature of the disease. Lowered resistance and a body not working properly predispose an individual to disease. Identifying the type of micro-organism will help determine whether it is bacteria, viral or both. The type of environmental pollutant will determine whether it is cancer, black lung, asbestos poisoning, etc. The practice of medicine has built its approach to disease upon the characteristic of the disease. Medicine addresses its attention to the nature of the disease and then decides whether to ignore it, treat it, remove it or prevent it.

Summary of Disease Factors

1 Primary factors create an inability: an inability of the body to function as it should. Limitations of the body and incoordination of its function are the two most apparent causes of functional inability. Heredity is the most common cause of limitations of the body and interference in the nervous system, which we will discuss in a future chapter, is the most common cause of incoordination.

2 Secondary factors create an inadequacy: an inadequacy to meet our body's needs. You must determine what resources are adequate for your body. You must use your educated intelligence to note the desires of the innate intelligence with regard to sufficient rest, exercise, nutrition and proper mental attitude. If you don't get a sufficient amount, your body will be inadequate to meet its needs. Secondary factors also depend upon the ability of the individual to use the rest, exercise, etc. that it receives. For example, vitamins that the body is unable to assimilate become inadequate. Many people take in a sufficient amount of vitamins but the body is unable to utilize them because of a primary factor.

3 Tertiary factors are related to an invasion. If your body is to remain healthy in the presence of these tertiary factors, it must have the ability to withstand their invasion (primary), and have *sufficient* resources to withstand their invasive character (secondary factors).

Primary factors deal with the body's potential. Without potential, nothing else matters. If you do not have the genetic potential to reach a high level of health, nothing will enable you to reach that level. If your body is working in an incoordinated manner (due to vertebral subluxation for example - a subject we shall discuss shortly) and you are lacking the potential to turn good food into healthy tissue, the most nourishing food will be of no benefit. Potential is primary.

Secondary factors deal with the body's resources. Resources deal with what you give your body to work with; food, water, exercise and positive mental attitudes are the natural resources that the body with the proper potential can turn into health. Just because we have called them secondary in no way demeans or lessens their importance. Secondary factors are vital and are each individual's personal responsibility. Once the potential is there, having the necessary resources becomes an important factor.

Tertiary factors deal with the body's environment. Environment is important, however, it is of less importance than the others simply because there is very little we as individuals can do to affect it. That is largely the difference between the outside-in approach and the above-down approach. The outside-in approach tries to change the environment without really knowing what it should be or how to properly balance it. The above-down approach is to enable us to better adapt to that environment no matter what it is. With sufficient potential and sufficient resources, the body under normal circumstances adapts to its environment.

The real point to be made in this entire discussion is that it is foolish to try to find causes for disease because there are so many primary, secondary and tertiary factors involved that the entire issue of cause is unclear. As we said, disease causation is like the saying "the straw that broke the camel's back." Was the *last* straw really the cause? It was no more the cause than the first straw or all the factors in between. If it were the cause, it alone would have caused the camel's "spinal fracture." All of them are factors. The health and strength of the camel was also a factor. In a system like the human body where there are so many variables and so many factors, it becomes impossible to make absolute statements such as single causes of disease. This is not to say that there are not absolutes within the body and the world and there are not single causes. But when it comes to disease, the idea of single cause just does not fit.

In a health-raising (ADIO) approach, causes of disease are not even a consideration. As a side-effect of a health-raising approach, we often see people get well from their diseases. This of course is important to the people who are sick. Let's examine the mechanism by which this happens.

•   •   •   •   •   •   •   •   •   •   •   •

10

WHY A HEALTH-RAISING APPROACH GETS PEOPLE WELL

Since disease results from a lowered level of health unique to each individual, people do get well under health care, depending upon whether the health level can be raised above the disease level. If the health level can be raised sufficiently, they are cured. If not, they do not get well. Sometimes health-raising measures are not sufficient to bring up the level, especially if the individual is only improving in one or two health-raising areas. If a person is going to get the maximum health benefit, he or she should not do it halfway. Starting to eat well without exercising misses the whole point. You need to eat properly, exercise regularly and do all the other activities necessary to health.

Health is the Entity

The fact that people do or do not get well from health-raising measures is another indication that it is not disease which is the entity but health. If it were disease, then diet, exercise, drugs or other therapeutic procedures, if they worked at all, would work all the time. The disease supposedly doesn't change from one person to another, nor does the drug with which it is being treated. If the assumption were made that disease is not the same in all people, then the entire concept of using one drug for a disease would have no merit. The field of medicine assumes that the same disease in different people is the same. They give the same vaccination to all people to prevent disease. They have a standard procedure for every disease implying that, for the most part, disease is standardized. The only time they alter their procedure is when the person has more than one disease. If every disease were unique to the individual, the entire theory of drug therapy would be rejected. The truth is that the *health level* in every person where the disease occurs is different. On occasions, medical therapy will alter its standard procedures because it recognizes this very fact. People with the same disease may have a very different health level. They may say "he is not strong enough to handle this procedure" or "this drug is the best treatment but her condition is such that it would be too strong for her." They recognize that everyone's health level is different, even those with the same disease, but they continue, for the most part, to treat every disease with the same drugs.

The ability of an individual person to get well of a disease is not the potency or the effectiveness of the drug or medical procedure but the ability of the body to raise the health level above the disease manifestation level at the same time that therapeutic measures are being taken. If it were the drug alone that made the difference, every person would get well from the drug regardless of their health level. An elderly person with the flu would respond to treatment as quickly as a 10-year-old child. Usually, along with any therapeutic measure, the individual will consciously or unconsciously begin health-raising measures. Proper rest is necessary to maintaining health, so the individual confined to bed is raising his/her health level. Drinking fluids and eating wholesome foods are other measures taken during an illness. Perhaps they temporarily suspend health-lowering measures, such as eating junk food, foods with chemicals, additives and preservatives, drinking alcohol and/or long hours at a stress-related job. These measures will also raise the health level. The person raises the health level, often sufficiently enough to cure the disease.

Surgery, to remove a diseased organ, in a sense gets rid of the disease but does nothing to raise the health level. In fact, it reduces the health level further,

> You cannot be as healthy as you should be without organs that were meant to be there

for a necessary organ of the body has been removed. However, the disease may disappear. The worst part of this procedure is that the individual probably believes that he or she is healthier when in fact the health level is reduced further than it was before the surgery. You cannot be as healthy as you should be without organs that were meant to

• • • • • • • • • • • • • • •

be there. This is not to imply that on occasions surgery is not necessary. However, even if necessary to preserve the life of the individual, his/her health level is still reduced by whatever value that organ may have had to health. What is worse, the level can never be increased to the potential it would be if the organ was still there, functioning, and all other factors were equal.

Health Restoration vs. Disease Treatment

It is important to understand that health restoration to someone with a disease is different than treating that disease. There are philosophical differences.

In treating the disease, if the health level has not been raised, the disease will return. This is commonly seen in infections. The antibiotic will, in effect, destroy the micro-organism (temporarily plug the hole), but the health level is so low and the vitality of the tissue so depleted that when the drug is eliminated from the person's body, the bacteria once again set up housekeeping. Unless the body's natural defense mechanisms are able to function properly, the disease will return and those mechanisms can only function at a certain health level.

In addition, health restoration always has a positive effect. Disease treatment, on the other hand, almost always is adding something to the body that is not naturally or normally there. It must decrease the health level even if it is treating the disease. The proof of this point can be clearly made by an experiment or by simple logic. If you administer a drug or medication to a healthy person long enough, eventually you will make them sick. It reduces their health level. If you administer it to a sick person, even if it relieves the symptom or, in the case of an antibiotic, kills the germ, it still reduces their health level. If that level is low enough to begin with, the drug may kill them or make them worse and if nothing is done at the same time to raise their health level, they will not improve. It is not the drug or the disease then that determines whether an individual improves, gets worse or stays the same. It is a function of their health level and how it is changing or not changing during the course of the disease.

CHILDHOOD DISEASES

An understanding of health,
an appreciation for the body's ability to heal itself and a
general knowledge of the ADIO philosophy is nowhere more
evident and necessary than when it comes to children and the
results of a lack of health that affect them. It seems that we
as adults are willing to suffer more and persevere longer with
conditions that affect us. Sometimes we are willing to persevere too long before having them corrected. But when it
comes to children, it is a good deal more difficult. Problems
that we would ignore or let run their course we are prone to
seek treatment for in a child. This is especially true when the
child is too young to communicate how they feel.

Disease, whether occurring in childhood or adulthood,
occurs for the same reason. It is the result of a lowered health
level. Many micro-organisms are normally present in the air

we breathe. When the health level drops to a certain point, they invade the body and the signs and symptoms of the disease result. Often the child appears to have extreme symptoms, more extreme than would an adult with the same condition. It is partly because the child is young and even though his or her health level has dropped, he or she still possesses the ability to react and respond to outside forces more vigorously than an adult. Sometimes parents are overly concerned and symptoms are exaggerated in their minds. As the years go by the child's ability to respond better will likely be reduced. We tend to desensitize our innate response system as we get older, somewhat like developing calluses on the hands. When you irritate the skin, it responds by causing discomfort, to tell you to remove the irritant. If you do not remove it, then the body says "okay, we must adapt the best we can, we will build tougher but insensitive tissue." Infants respond innately to many things. If they drink too much milk, they will bring it up. They don't find it socially unacceptable to soil a diaper. If they are hot, cold or tired, they let everybody know. They have food likes and dislikes. Because of this ability to respond vigorously, their response to the microbes in the environment tends to be extreme. Vomiting and fever are two examples. It takes very little to cause children to vomit or run a fever.

> Children tend to react strongly, but they also bounce back quickly

While children tend to react strongly, they also have the ability to bounce back quickly. Every parent has experienced a child on his or her "deathbed" at 8 AM on a school day that was ready to go out and play before noon. Now sometimes it is a desire to play hooky but often the child really is better in a few hours. Everything else being equal, the younger the body the greater the ability to heal itself and bounce back.

There are two other factors that we must consider with childhood diseases. The first is that children's health levels have a tendency to have greater fluctuation than adults. (The smaller the container, the greater the evidence of the level drop.) A gallon of water removed from Lake Michigan will not be nearly as evident as a gallon of water removed from a 2 1/2 gallon bucket. So when the child misses a good night's sleep or eats poorly for a day or two, his or her body reacts in a more extreme manner. The second factor is related to the first in that the body builds immunity to certain diseases as time goes on and it has the experience of fighting off the disease. Immunity is the body learning how to fight off disease. In essence the body has a limited ability to plug up some of its own holes until it learns by experience. It develops the antibodies and other necessary factors and each time the body comes in contact with the micro-organism, it responds appropriately. It takes an experience to learn that process. This immunity adds to the health level. It tends to reduce the drastic loss of health when coming in contact with the natural micro-organisms of our environment. Immunity, then, is a level-stabilizing factor by reducing the effect of environmental micro-organisms, making the bucket less susceptible to holes. Every time you get the flu you develop immunity to that particular virus. The problem is that viruses change so quickly (adapt and evolve) that you can never become immune to them all. But the organisms that cause

•   •   •   •   •   •   •   •   •   •   •   •   •

childhood diseases are more specific so the child reacts upon his or her initial contact with the organism and then develops a permanent immunity.

It is more than just a coincidence that under normal circumstances a childhood disease causes very little complications when occurring in a child. The child's body has greater ability to raise its health level, often during an initial exposure and reaction. Complications in children only occur when the child's health level is extremely low. The key word is extremely. The infrequency of childhood disease complications indicates that the child's health level must be below the vast majority of children. However, these diseases, when occurring in adulthood, can have very serious complications. Rubella during the first trimester of pregnancy can seriously affect the fetus. Mumps in adulthood can lead to sterility. Apparently, the human body was designed to experience these diseases in childhood, not in adulthood.

Childhood diseases are not pleasant. No sickness is pleasant. But childhood is the time to get them. All diseases, while not pleasant, have a positive survival value to them. Childhood diseases build immunity. Immunity reduces the health-lowering tendency of micro-organisms in the environment. It reduces the size of the hole in the bucket naturally so in effect, reduces health loss and has the effect of raising the health level. Childhood diseases are valuable experiences. The key is to have the child's body at a high enough level of health that it can handle the disease and make it a positive, health-raising (immunity-building) experience. The field of medicine has seen the health-raising effects of immunity and has attempted to artificially duplicate the process by vaccination. Trying to educatedly plug up holes when that is the role of the innate intelligence of the body is not raising the individual's level of health.

The Immune System

Most systems in the body can be easily described and delineated. As a system, they are usually large enough to be visible to the naked eye. The cardiovascular system is very extensive. The digestive system extends from the mouth to the anus. The immune system of the body however, is an "ill"-defined system within the body. It is made up of organs, glands, and structures and the chemicals produced by those organs and glands. Its purpose is to defend us against invasive organisms and to destroy anything foreign to the body. It is responsible for destroying cancer cells before they can reproduce. It also is the reason why the body tends to reject organ transplants. Anything foreign to the body is attacked by the immune system. However, the immune system can be overcome with drugs. The sad side effect of this for organ transplant recipients is that the success of these drugs also causes the individual to have greater tendency to develop cancer, which is a very common cause of death among transplant recipients.

Like other systems of the body, the immune system's ability to function depends upon the health level of the body and also what is done directly to the organ. Anything that will lower the health level of the body will affect every system including the immune system. When the health level is lowered, every tissue in the body is adversely affected. There are certain traumas and stresses that also directly affect certain systems. For example, smoking will affect all the systems of the body, including the respiratory system because it reduces the overall health level of the body. Additionally, smoking will directly traumatize the respiratory system by damaging the lungs. Alcohol affects the entire body to a degree but has a direct traumatic effect upon the liver. The factors that affect the health level of the body indirectly affect the immune system, whether they *directly* affect it or not. Research has shown that stress directly affects the immune system. The system is strengthened by being used and used properly like every other system of the body. If it is abused, it is weakened. What is beneficial use and what is abuse? That will depend, to a great degree, on the health of the system and the health of the body.

Vaccinations

The health of the immune system is the issue surrounding vaccination. Is the immune system of the body able to handle the natural, normal exposures to an organism or is it limited in its ability and in need of outside help? Those that hold to an ADIO philosophy believe that the body can handle its natural environment and that so-called "help" by vaccination is actually contrary to natural laws and does more harm than good. Not to mention that no one drug's effects can be adequately or accurately predicted for any single individual as previously mentioned. Those that hold to an outside-in philosophy believe the body is limited and needs help, needs a boost to cause the system to work. Those that hold to an ADIO philosophy believe the body can handle its natural environment. However, the environment has been made unnatural to a degree. The body has a fantastic ability to heal and keep itself healthy. But it is limited. Who is correct?

Like every issue of health, vaccination is an individual decision. Some people may believe that their body is limited in its natural immune ability and needs help. They fear the organisms in the environment more than they fear the dangers of immunization. They may even believe that the unnatural way that we have affected the environment has created a situation in which extreme educated measures should be taken. An example would be chlorinating our drinking water. Their fear of the pollutants in the water is greater than their confidence in the body's ability to withstand those pollutants. Others have confidence in their body's ability to maintain health in the environment and their fear of vaccinations is greater than their fear of the micro-organism.

People should have the freedom and the right to make decisions regarding their health. No government should deprive them of that freedom. Whatever the decision you make, you should make sure that everything possible is being done to raise and maintain your health level or your child's. If one does not want to depend upon artificial immunization, he or she should keep the body as healthy as possible to withstand the environmental forces. If one does decide on vaccination, then the body needs to be as healthy as possible to handle the poison introduced into the body and thereby minimizing its harmful side-effects.

•   •   •   •   •   •   •   •   •   •   •   •

12

CHIROPRACTIC CARE

We have saved
what we believe is the most important contribution to your
health level until now, partly because this book is not about
chiropractic. It is about health. While all the health-raising
measures are important, there is a measure that stands apart
because it is the basis for determining the effectiveness of all
the others. Chiropractic is probably the most misunderstood
profession in the history of the health field in spite of its
100-year history and the number of people who utilize the
services of a chiropractor. It is, however, a very simple
philosophy. It is part of the larger ADIO world and life view
which we have been examining. Sadly, the majority of the
people who come under chiropractic care do so not from an
ADIO perspective but from an outside-in below-up viewpoint. They are really seeking outside-in care and have

assumed that chiropractic is part of that mode of care. It may seem to some that it really does not matter how you view chiropractic as long as you are benefiting from chiropractic care. While it is true that some benefit occurs, if you are not fitting chiropractic into your ADIO viewpoint, its benefit will be limited.

Some Use Chiropractic to Treat Conditions

The sole purpose of this book is to encourage you toward a correct perspective regarding your health, whether it involves chiropractic, medicine, diet, exercise or anything else, so that you may receive maximum benefit. I believe having that right perspective does matter. It is like the difference between using a television as a plant stand or tapping into 181 channels of potential entertainment. It may make a beautiful plant stand. But hook up the cable, plug it in, and turn it on and the television will become much more valuable to you. (Of course, that is based upon the assumption that anything on television is of value.) Too many people use chiropractic as a plant stand and not enough are "plugged" into its real value. Some people use chiropractic to get rid of the symptoms of a medical condition. They go to a chiropractor for headaches, backaches, sinus trouble, allergies or other conditions they believe (or have been told) can be helped by chiropractic care. Sometimes they get well and sometimes they do not. But either way they have missed the true benefit of chiro-

> They miss the true benefit of chiropractic and they have not seen the ADIO philosophy within it

practic care and they have not seen the ADIO philosophy within it. They have, in fact, used chiropractic as an outside-in approach to the treatment of their disease or condition. They have not understood the simple philosophy of chiropractic and hence have missed its far-reaching benefits and applications.

Perhaps it should be noted at this point that not only can chiropractic be used by the patient in an outside-in manner but it can be practiced by the chiropractor in that manner. This may occur for economic reasons. The medical approach to treating disease has always been the most lucrative in the healing arts. It may occur because the chiropractor himself has never understood the ADIO philosophy of chiropractic or it may occur because the chiropractor has decided he wants to be part of the mainstream of health care delivery and not go against accepted thought. This book will present chiropractic from the ADIO viewpoint. While there may be times when we will be critical of the outside-in approach to health care and use examples of medicine, the intent of this book, we want to reiterate, is not to tell you what to do and what not to do but to give you information and allow you to make a decision for yourself.

Some Use ADIO Principles to Treat Disease

The above-down inside-out and outside-in below-up viewpoints are totally different in their approach and their results. Health restoration is above-down inside-out, disease treatment is outside-in below-up. Unfortunately, many approaches to health restoration are also used as approaches to disease treatment. The practitioner may be using the

•   •   •   •   •   •   •   •   •   •   •   •   •

OIBU approach by intent, but in doing so, is setting into motion certain ADIO principles. Rest is important to maintain health. Rest is also used to treat diseases from the common cold to cancer. The doctor tells the patient to go home and stay in bed for 48 hours. His intention is to treat the disease. However, in going to bed, the patient sets into motion certain health-restoring principles. Bacteria and viruses do not die when a person is placed in the horizontal position. Rest does not affect them. But rest restores life and vitality to the individual and that gets them well.

Proper eating is necessary to maintain health. Special diets are also used in treating diseases like heart disease, diabetes and gall bladder disease. Good eating is above-down inside-out; nutritional therapy is outside-in. Exercise is a part of health maintenance. It is also used for rehabilitation of heart disease and stroke victims. The most valuable aspect of chiropractic is as a health-maintaining and health-restoring measure. As such, like rest, exercise and proper nutrition, it is valuable to every member of the human race. That is the first principle. Chiropractic care is for everyone. Used as a disease treatment however, it has very limited application and minimum benefits. As an analogy, nutrition therapy does not help some heart patients. On the other hand, good eating habits benefit everyone because everyone can be healthier if they eat better. In some, improvement may not be noticed but it is there. It is sad to think that there are millions of people using chiropractic as a treatment for diseases like headaches, allergies, sinus trouble and back pains when its application to health is so much more beneficial. It is like using a pair of Stradivarius violins

•   •   •   •   •   •   •   •   •   •   •   •   •

as bookends! They may look beautiful on the shelf and keep the books upright, but what a waste!

Chiropractic is based upon the simple principle that the body naturally strives toward health. This striving is an expression of the innate intelligence of the body. The nervous system is the primary system that the body uses in this striving. If one of the bones of the spine becomes misaligned (subluxated), the nervous system is interfered with and this striving toward health and harmonious function is lessened. Simply put, the body, whatever its state of health or level of health, is better off with a good nerve supply. The body can work in the presence of vertebral subluxation but it cannot work as well, the health level will be reduced. Most important, the contribution made by diet, exercise, and rest is lessened. Subluxations occur all the time in every person at all ages. They can first occur at the moment of birth and unless corrected, they rob the body of its ability to be healthy. The chiropractic objective is the correction of vertebral subluxation in all members of the human race. Young, old, apparently sick, or apparently healthy, everyone can benefit from chiropractic care. Often, when subluxations are corrected in sick people, their diseases seem to disappear. This has caused people to believe that chiropractic is an effective treatment for those diseases. We are presenting chiropractic in this book as something other than a treatment for disease.

Chiropractic care is part of the health picture, like diet, exercise and rest, but it occupies a special place. Eating good food is not a substitute for exercise or getting the proper rest. Exercise is not an alternative to hygiene or a good mental

• • • • • • • • • • • •

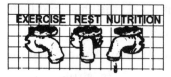

attitude. Each one is part of the health picture. Chiropractic is unique among the others. It is the glue that holds them all together or, in following our bucket analogy, the funnel that blends them together and deposits them into the body as this entity called "health."

Diet is important. The body cannot live on donuts and coffee. It needs good food to make healthy tissue. But it also must have the ability to use that food, to make it into walking, talking flesh and blood. You could put the most nutritious meal ever made into the mouth and stomach of a corpse and it will not become living tissue. It needs life to make it usable and of benefit to the body. If life is lacking in the living body due to vertebral subluxation, the food, as good as it might be, will be of less or little value.

Exercise is an integral part of health. However, exercising muscles fibers that are deprived of a good nerve supply due to subluxation is not as beneficial. A physical therapist may exercise the muscles of someone who is paralyzed, however, the therapist's efforts do not help those muscle fibers that have no nerve supply. The exercise will only benefit the muscles where the damage to the nervous system has not occurred. The hope is that they will be able to make up for the muscles deprived of a good nerve supply.

•   •   •   •   •   •   •   •   •   •   •   •   •

Sometimes it helps, often it does not. You can exercise muscles all you want but if they are not receiving a full supply of life through the nervous system, there is less or little benefit.

Rest is important to the repair of tissues and the body in general. But unless the body is working properly, the rest will be of minimal value. Subluxation robs the body of the benefits of rest. Everyone has had the experience of getting their usual night's sleep but not waking up refreshed and rested. The hours asleep did not produce the desired results. The chemical changes that must take place within the body while sleeping will not occur if the glands and organs producing those chemicals do not have a good nerve supply.

The part of the brain that is responsible for mental attitude is greatly affected by the chemistry of the body. This is apparent by the simple fact that drugs, both legal and illicit, are taken to alter the mood of an individual. If the nervous system is not functioning properly, the organs and glands that manufacture chemicals to balance the body's chemistry will not function properly. You may be short-tempered or feeling stressed because of improper body chemistry.

All the components of health are necessary, and none is a substitute for another, but chiropractic care is necessary to receive the maximum benefits of all of them.

If there is one final principle with regard to health-raising factors that needs to be understood and applied, it is the principle of consistency. Almost anything done with a measure of success in every aspect of life is done on a consistent basis. The more consistency in your life, the more

• • • • • • • • • • • • •

successful you will become. There is a difference between "consistency" and "habit." Developing an habitual program in any area of health, that is, not being flexible, is denying the dynamics of the human body and its needs, and is actually a hindrance to health. We need to be consistent without being habitual. We need to consistently eat well-balanced meals but not the same foods at every meal, day-in and day-out. We need to have a consistent exercise program but one that varies according to our daily needs. Getting into a rut is not healthful. It deprives the individual of being adaptable in their mental attitude. Being consistent, on the other hand, is a quality to be desired and worked toward.

Vertebral Subluxation

A vertebral subluxation is the physical representation of a cause of a lack of health in the human body, at least the cause that the chiropractor addresses. Notice we do not say it is a cause of a *disease* but a cause of a *lack of health* and a lack of health is a primary cause of disease, as we have already discussed. So while this cause of a lack of health is not the cause of any particular disease, it is a cause of every disease. Very simply, in every disease known to man, a single common denominator is a body that is not working properly. A subluxation is a misalignment of one of the bones (vertebrae) of the spine, which interferes with the function of the nervous system. The purpose of these bones is to house and protect the vital and delicate nerves that supply the life-giving energy to every part of the body. Due to this close proximity and the nature of bone and nerves, when the vertebrae misalign or subluxate, they become the greatest insult to the very nerves they are supposed to protect. When an interference occurs, the body begins to work at less than its fullest potential. A body functioning at less than its fullest potential has lost, among other things, some of its health. What makes chiropractic unique is the recognition of and attention to the vertebral subluxation. The subluxation is the focus of a chiropractic practice because it interferes with the full expression of the innate intelligence of the body. Whether some people believe it is a cause of back pain, scoliosis, any disease or all diseases is not relevant to the chiropractic health maintenance practice. It is an interference to the full expression of life within the body and other than the chiropractor, there is no one who makes a practice of intentionally correcting subluxations. The surgeon may inadvertently do it while performing spinal surgery. The orthopedist may unknowingly correct one when applying traction to the patient's spine. The family physician may enable the body to correct one by telling the patient to go home, drink fluids and get plenty of rest. But the chiropractor is the only one purposefully doing it every day and on every patient.

Are subluxations so bad? Obviously the medical profession, if they acknowledge the existence of subluxations at all, does not place much emphasis upon the harm they do to the human body, otherwise they would be correcting them. The subluxation has been likened to a rubber band around the tip of your finger. It doesn't really hurt. It may not be causing a problem, except that it is cutting off the circulation to the end of your finger. Can you live with that? Sure, just not as well. Just being the tip of your finger, it probably will not drastically affect your daily performance. However, eventually problems within the finger tip would occur. Lack of blood could cause cell damage. It could lead to gangrene which, if ignored, could lead to blood poisoning which could cause death. Here's the question. When do you want to remove the rubber band from your finger? When you are at the point of death? When they surgically remove the gangrenous finger? When it becomes numb? How about right away... as soon as you realize that it is not good for your body to be walking around with a rubber band wrapped tightly around your finger? That's when you want to have a vertebral subluxation corrected... right away. We do not know how much damage it is doing to the body. But we can conclude that since the body was not meant to be subluxated, it is doing damage and it is not good to allow your body to be walking around with a damaged nervous system.

Why Does the Body Subluxate?

The question is often raised, "if the body is as great and wonderful as we say, why does it subluxate? The body does have a tremendous ability to withstand the forces that subluxate the spine, but it does have limitations. It can withstand the force of stepping off a curb, but a fall off the back porch will probably subluxate it. A subluxation occurs because an outside force (an external, invasive force) overcomes the resistance (internal forces) of the body. The body can resist the force of stepping off the curb, but the fall off the back porch is greater than it can handle.

There are forces that we are subjected to every day, forces that our body is perfectly capable of handling. Every step of walking jolts the spine, but the body can easily absorb that force. Sitting down, putting our head on the pillow at night, bending over to tie our shoes, all subject the spine to a force and all under normal circumstances are easily adapted to by the body. The body contracts certain muscles during these activities that stabilize the vertebrae, preventing them from becoming subluxated. This action occurs innately, without any thought on our part. However, there are certain forces that can overcome it no matter how well the body adapts. That our muscles have limitations is not a difficult concept to understand. Certain objects are just too heavy to lift. That is a limitation of muscles.

Perhaps the very first external force that created a subluxation in you was during your own birth. Even a natural, uncomplicated delivery creates stress upon the child's spine (not to mention the mother's). Under normal circumstances the baby's spine is able to handle this stress. However, deliveries in which the mother is not prepared, not in the best position to deliver, or in which the doctor pulls and twists the baby's head and neck can result in subluxation of the spine. A lengthy labor will stress the infant's entire body, including the spine. A newborn's muscles are not strong enough to handle these forces. The subluxation that occurs may remain until and unless a chiropractor corrects it. It most definitely will remain until another force is introduced to the spine in such a way as to set that bone in motion toward the correct position. Most often the hands of a chiropractor are the most specific and effective method. Although it is conceivable that a fall down a flight of steps could "adjust" the bone back into its proper position. (It is more likely that a vertebra would be subluxated in such a fall.) It is sad to think of the millions of babies that are subluxated and never get to a chiropractor or at least do not get to one until it is too late and permanent damage to the nervous system and the tissues it supplies has occurred and the health level has been reduced to a level from which it will never rise.

If the young child is not subluxated at birth, surely he or she will be subluxated as they are handled by everybody, passed from relative to relative. When they are learning to stand and walk, they may fall twenty times a day, constantly introducing forces into their small spines. They fall out of bed, off the couch, off their bicycles, while rollerskating, running and playing. Now they are even playing contact sports like football as early as seven years old. The amazing thing is that a child has *any* vertebrae *in* place by the time they are ten. They are constantly subjected to external invasive forces. Every child should have the spine checked regularly from birth onward. By adjusting the spine the child's body has greater capacity to seal off the "holes" (in the bucket analogy) associated with environmental stress. That is why children under chiropractic care often seem to bounce back faster from illness than adults and other children. The body's ability to raise its health level is naturally better in children and enhanced by chiropractic adjustments.

Forces that Subluxate

The forces that subluxate the spine fall into three general categories.

Physical. These are the most easily understood. Falls, automobile accidents and other traumas are the most common. The force of these traumas will overcome the stabilizing work of muscles, ligaments and the natural tendency for the spine to remain in its proper position. What are not as easily recognized but probably more common are the minimal or microforces that the body is subjected to every day. These physical forces, which often go unnoticed, will, under certain circumstances, cause one or more of the vertebrae of the spine to subluxate. Sitting at an architect's drawing board all day or awkwardly filling cavities in a dental office creates subliminal or imperceptible forces. Sitting at a computer terminal, holding the phone between the shoulder and the chin, bending over an automobile engine, or sitting in a cab or truck all day are other examples. Most occupations today involve one or two repetitive activities. These can lead to vertebral subluxation if the body does not have the capacity to adapt. Some sports such as tennis, golf, racquet ball and other "one-armed" activities as well as other common, every day occurrences (crossing your legs the same way, carrying your purse on the same shoulder) can have the same effect.

Chemical. As a cause of invasive forces, chemicals are not so easily understood. The chemicals (poisons) that we put into our body affect every tissue and cell in our body including our nervous system and our muscles. Certain poisons directly affect the nerve system and others directly affect muscles. But all of them have some affect upon these systems. There is a principle that applies here which we have discussed earlier. A principle true in the visible realm is also true in the non-visible realm. If a brick is dropped into a bucket of water, the level of the water rises in direct proportion to the mass of the brick. Archimedes is said to have discovered this principle in his bathtub. As we have mentioned before, the principle is no less true if the brick is dropped into Lake Michigan, although we cannot see the rise in the level of the lake. If chemicals such as preservatives, pesticides and hormones are taken into the body in large quantities, they will do damage. It follows then, that if they are taken into the body in small quantities, they will do damage even though not perceived or noticed. The damaging effects of these chemicals may be cumulative, that is, they may build up. While it is true that the body has the ability to eliminate some of the poisons, the body is limited in that ability and damage must occur. Reflex mechanisms in the nervous system can cause muscles to contract and lead to subluxation. Direct chemical influence on a muscle can cause it to contract and can lead to a subluxation. Lactic acid is a chemical produced in the body by muscle activity. If not removed, it can cause the contraction of muscles that we call cramps. If this happens to muscles surrounding the vertebrae, subluxations can occur.

3 *Emotional.* This factor has become a very important one in recent times. Everyone talks about stress and the toll it takes on the human body. Later in this book much more will be devoted to the subject; but emotions do create a stress upon the body which is manifested in tightness in the muscles and can result in subluxation.

Each of the above three external forces can cause subluxation. But the real danger is that together they have a cumulative effect upon the body and cause subluxations without the individual realizing that they are factors in decreasing their health. For example, an individual who may ordinarily adapt to sitting at a desk for eight hours may become subluxated because he has filled his body with chemicals and poisons in the form of coffee, alcohol and poor foods which he has consumed because he has been under great emotional stress. The combination of all of these causes the spine to subluxate. The individual really has not done anything significantly different but the cumulative effect of these external forces has caused vertebral subluxation. These types of subluxations are the real danger to the health of an individual because he is unaware of their occurrence and unaware of the toll they are taking upon his health. The subluxation that occurs as a result of a fall on an icy sidewalk, which is accompanied by pain, is a good one (if we can call a subluxation good). The person knows he has injured himself. He seeks care. Hopefully, he has learned enough about chiropractic to conclude that, in addition to the bumps or bruises and injury that may require medical attention, he may have subluxated himself. He goes to the chiropractor to have his spine checked. Subluxations caused by work, poisons and emotions may not be accompanied by any outward symptoms. These subluxations, however, are just as real and just as harmful to the person. The cause of the subluxation is not the issue. When it occurs, the body is deprived of its full complement of mental impulses and works at less than its fullest potential. This is why the chiropractor is anxious to regularly check every patient. There are no alarms, red lights or warning systems to tell you that subluxations which have caused no noticeable symptoms have occurred. Yet they are just as bad as the ones associated with severe trauma.

Why Can't the Body Correct Its Own Subluxations?

Another question asked is "Why doesn't the body correct these subluxations?" The majority of the time the body *does* correct its own subluxations. The muscles of the body very often do pull the vertebra back into place, taking the pressure off the nerves. But there are times when the muscles are not able to accomplish this task. If they are weak, full of toxins, or if the subluxation is depriving them of sufficient mental impulses (energy) to correct the subluxation, it will not happen.

The body is limited, even in its ability to correct its own vertebral subluxations. If this situation occurs, then an outside force, the hands of a chiropractor, is needed to correct the subluxation.

Preventing Subluxation

The key to preventing subluxation is very simple. It is just doing those things necessary to lead a healthy life. Eating properly, exercising regularly, avoiding poisons and stress and generally leading a common sense life. The more health conscious one is, the less the spine will tend to subluxate. None of us is perfect in our lifestyles. We will go out and overeat or eat the wrong things. When that occurs you just get back into the program of natural living. Circumstances in life do affect our ability to lead a healthy life, however, they should only act as infrequent and short interruptions. Going away on vacation may disrupt our exercise schedule. But once we return, we should pick up where we left off. Social engagements or work may cause us to lose sleep one or two nights. But we should get back to our normal routine after these brief interruptions. If there is something in your regular day-to-day schedule that prevents you from doing those activities that will keep you healthy, then perhaps you need to re-evaluate your life and your lifestyle. Only in doing these activities and doing them consistently will the body work at a high enough level to withstand the day-to-day external forces that cause vertebral subluxations. But, as noted above, we are not perfect and we must realize that every time our life deviates from what is normal for us, an abnormal situation occurs and this gives rise to vertebral subluxations.

Failing to get the proper rest will reflect itself in vertebral subluxations. Getting "back into the program" may begin to raise your health level with regard to those components, but it will not correct the vertebral subluxations any more than getting back up after a fall will correct the subluxation that the fall caused. Subluxations remain because the body does not have the wherewithal to correct them. There is interference in the nervous system and the muscles directed by that nervous system cannot adjust the subluxation. Because of this, chiropractic spinal checks are needed regularly. The body has nutritional reserves so that if your diet is lacking for a day or two, the health level does not drop to the point of having signs and symptoms of disease, provided that all the other health factors are continually contributing to your health level. Similarly, if you miss a day or two of exercise, your body can handle it, provided that the other areas are still contributing to your health level. The same is true for rest. But while the health level may not drop to a level of disease, the body's ability to maintain itself free of subluxation is seriously impaired and there is no margin for error or safety valve with regard to the human spine. Any stress (physical, chemical, emotional) or a lack of performing health-maintaining measures takes it toll on the spine. It will often result in vertebral subluxation. That is why it is so necessary to have the spine checked on a regular basis. Getting back to good eating habits, getting back to exercise and getting back to good rest habits will enable you to replenish your health after "falling off the health wagon." But there is nothing the individual can do to restore spinal integrity except go to his or her chiropractor. If we led "perfect lives," we probably would not subluxate. But we don't, and whenever we slip either physically, chemically, emotionally or in maintaining health-promoting measures we will subluxate and we will need to be adjusted.

13

ENHANCE YOUR LIFE EXPERIENCE

This book has focused
on the subject of health and the above-down inside-out viewpoint of it. Perhaps it is time we expanded the area a little and discussed another area, specifically the area of human potential. If one is to truly enhance their life experience, then they most assuredly want to reach their potential in every aspect of their life. We have discussed the interrelationship of the body's parts, how each one is dependent upon the other, how health is a state of proper bodily function and how a lack of health, contrary to prevailing thought in orthodox medicine, does not just affect one part of the body but in fact reduces the function and the well-being of the entire body. When we discuss the subject of health we are really discussing the proper function of the body in every way, including the potential of the individual to make the

most of every aspect of his or her life experience. Everything is connected within the body and all you do is dependent upon your health. A television commercial aired a few years back in which the mother suffering from a headache was screaming at the children and snapping at her husband. Later (seconds on the commercial), thanks to the aspirin she took, she was a sweet, loving mother and wife.

While this is perhaps a distorted picture of reality, as is most of television, it demonstrates the principle that how we act and relate to people is dependent upon our state of health. Winston Churchill is reported to have said that "most of what is accomplished in this world is accomplished by people who do not feel well." That may be true, but it is a sad indictment upon the health-care delivery system in this world to realize that fact. Imagine what could be accomplished if all those people who don't feel well, did. A book written a few years ago entitled *Napoleon's Glands* analyzed Napoleon Bonaparte's strategy tactics and actions at the Battle of Waterloo and concluded that the usually brilliant military genius "met his Waterloo" because of physical problems including eczema, digestive problems and hemorrhoids. If this theory is true, the history of Europe and perhaps Western civilization was changed because one man did not feel well!

One's ability to function in the workplace depends upon his or her state of health. The employee who demonstrates energy and vitality and who does not miss work due to sickness has a better chance of advancement than the fellow who cannot stay awake during staff meetings. The healthier you are, the greater your ability to achieve and the further you will go in your career or business. Many businesses are realizing the importance of such things as exercise programs, nutritional meals and chiropractic care for their executives, and even for their employees. The very length of your life and how much you can accomplish in a lifetime is related to how healthy you are. It is not just luck or good fortune that many people lead long and productive lives, while others accomplish very little and live a relatively short time. There are some who accomplish a tremendous amount in a short life-span, but, as great a composer as Wolfgang Amadeus Mozart was in his short tragic life, imagine what he could have accomplished had he been healthy and lived a long, productive life.

Reaching your potential in life is largely a matter of balance. We use various terms to describe it. D.D. Palmer, the discoverer of chiropractic, in his book, *The Chiropractors Adjustor*, written in 1910 referred to it as "tone." The word used by many today is "homeostasis," a big word for "balance." The first thing that needs to be in balance is the chemistry of the body. The body is composed of billions upon billions of cells producing chemicals necessary to carry on every bodily function. We cannot wake up in the morning unless our body produces certain chemicals. That's why some people need a cup of coffee to get going in the morning. It supplies a chemical, caffeine, which is a stimulant. It is supposed to replace the chemicals that the body should be but apparently is not producing. We need chemicals to digest our breakfast, to react quickly when somebody cuts us off in the morning, rush-hour traffic. Our body must produce chemicals to enable us to think during the work day, to digest

•　•　•　•　•　•　•　•　•　•　•　•

lunch and negotiate the rush-hour traffic on the way home. Our body produces chemicals to handle stress and chemicals to enable us to fall asleep at night. People who are producing an insufficient amount have trouble sleeping and often take a chemical in the form of a drug to enable them to fall asleep. Those whose bodies are not producing chemicals to handle stress take a tranquilizer or some other form of chemical. But the drug makers or the drug takers really have no idea how much the body needs.

We fail to realize how delicate this balance is. Many people have been reminded by having a late evening cup of coffee and then spending half the night staring at the bedroom ceiling. The chemical balance of the body is a delicate thing. In addition to the production of chemicals, it is dependent upon taking the appropriate chemicals into the body in the form of food and, of course, not taking inappropriate chemicals like drugs and poisons. It is dependent upon all the systems using the chemicals, and it is dependent upon the nervous system as the tool to coordinate and control all of these functions. Chemical balance is necessary to health and reaching your potential.

Balancing your health-raising factors and your health-lowering factors is essential to health. Making sure that the health level is where it should be and is being maintained is of primary importance. Life is largely a matter of maintaining a balance to keep the health level where it should be. Those things that we do to add to our health level must equal or surpass those factors that are reducing it. And as we have seen, there are certain factors that will continually take more and more of our health, factors that we have no control over, like age and environment. It therefore behooves us to be doing those health-promoting activities more and more and always endeavoring to keep that health level balanced.

There must be a balance among the health-promoting factors. As we mentioned earlier in this book, exercising too much is harmful and becomes stress. Even good exercise does not replace good eating habits or getting adjusted on a regular basis. Balancing our rest and activity is important. Our needs may constantly fluctuate but it is essential that we keep them in balance.

Lastly, we must keep our work and recreation in balance and we must keep our emotions in balance. It is not easy especially in our society today. We wonder how, with all the labor-saving devices and inventions to make life easier, the stress and the work of just living seems great. But we must work to bring about a balance in our life. Learn to laugh, learn to relax, learn to have fun. But remember, work is not bad, there is a time to be serious. Many of us need to get serious about our life and health. Some of us need to get serious about having fun. Find a balance in your life.

What Is Your Potential?

Sadly, none of us reaches our potential. We could all be more, do more, enjoy life more, be more of a blessing and help to our fellow man, bring more joy into our lives and the lives of those around us. Why don't we? Science tells us that we use approximately 10% of our brain capacity. We are told that the human body is capable of living 120 to 150 years and there are only a few people that reach the lower figure. The sad thing is that very few reach anywhere near it. With all of

the supposed success of medical science in the past generation, the average life span has been increased only a few
years, a relatively few.

What is your potential and how can you know and reach
it? The first thing we need to address is our limitations. Yes,
we all have limitations. You are limited in the level of health
that you can reach. There are limitations within the human
body. Even Superman could not handle Kryptonite! The
human body has many limitations. It cannot withstand the
force of a .357 magnum bullet. It cannot handle a fall from
a ten-story building. It cannot overcome the effects of strong
poisons. There are certain things it was not designed to
handle. That is a limitation of the matter, the material aspect
of the body. But we have been given an educated mind to
overcome some of these limitations. Bullet-proof vests
protect police officers. Inflated cushions protect stunt men
jumping from ten-story buildings. Warning labels protect us
from poisons.

The greatest real limitation of matter that we have from
a health standpoint is our heredity. We are not going to be
any healthier or live longer than we have been programmed.
We may never reach what we were programmed to live but
we most certainly will not exceed it. We may never use all
the features of a computer program but even if we do, we
will never get it to do something it was not designed to do.
The genetic abilities you have determine the outer limits,
limits that you cannot exceed. But, quite frankly, using that
limitation for not reaching your potential is as much of a
cop-out as blaming sickness and disease on heredity. If we
were doing all that we could do, then we might get away with

•   •   •   •   •   •   •   •   •   •   •   •   •

blaming it on heredity. When people try to blame their diseases on heredity, it usually is clear that they have failed to take responsibility for their own life and actions. If their health habits are questioned, it will usually come to light that they did not exercise regularly nor watch their diet and were not under regular chiropractic care. Yet, it is easier to place the blame elsewhere. I have a strong suspicion that if we did all that we could do, we would not want to place any blame. We would live long, productive, active lives and fulfill all our goals, wishes and plans. Let's apply some areas of human potential to our health.

One of the greatest baseball players ever to play the game was a man named Pete Rose. He had some personal problems after leaving the game but that cannot detract from his accomplishments on the field. What made Pete Rose great was that he probably came closer to reaching his potential than any man who played the game. He was not a man with tremendous natural ability as a baseball player but he realized that he had the potential to be great if he worked at it. He used his natural abilities to the maximum and then he used his head and his heart to take him further than any other man in certain facets of the game. He was a student of the game, he hustled as a habit, even when he did not have to. He developed tremendous concentration. In a crucial game of the 1980 World Series, while playing first base with the Phillies, he followed the catcher chasing a foul ball and when the ball popped out of the catchers mitt, he was right there to catch it before it touched the ground. Hustle and concentration were his greatest assets. If Pete Rose had attacked the game of baseball like most other players, he probably would have been a nobody. But he did not. He didn't cry and moan about his limitations of natural ability. He didn't sit in the dugout and say "if only I had the speed of Maury Wills, or the natural hitting ability of Rod Carew or the power of Mike Schmidt." He went out and drained every ounce out of his ability that he could, reached his potential and became one of the best-all around players in the history of the game. He removed distractions, interferences if you will, and got the most out of himself.

Before the "big men" began to dominate the game of basketball, rarely did a player dunk the ball. Even on a fast break all alone, they would lay it up. Did they not have the potential to do it? When I look up at a basket, I say to myself, how in the world do they do that? Then I look at the size of those guys and say "that's how!" Yet there is a professional basketball player who is exactly the same height as I am who can dunk a basketball. Spud Webb is 5'6" and can slam a basketball through a hoop 10 feet off the ground. It appears that no one ever told Spud that 5'6" guards don't dunk the ball. Does he have natural ability that I do not have that enables him to dunk the ball? Perhaps. But we will never know because I never put in the time, the effort or the energy to develop my body and my skills to learn to dunk a basketball. Maybe if I worked from now until the cows come home, I would never reach it. Maybe I would. I know one thing, if I worked as hard at it as Spud Webb did, whatever height or level I reached would certainly impress the other guys on Thursday nights at the gym.

My father has an acrylic painting in his home that he painted some years back. It is absolutely beautiful. It's a wooded scene with a small lake in the foreground and some mountains in the background. I am not an art critic but I think it's great. My father had never painted in his life or did anything of an artistic nature. He went to a class with his younger brother and at age 70, he with twenty-five other people in the class painted this picture. I asked him if everybody did as well. He said that everyone in the class, none of whom had any experience, painted the same scene. Some were a little better than his and some a little worse. The point is that every one of them had the potential to paint a picture that no one would be ashamed to hang on the wall in their home. Does that mean that every one of us has the potential to be an artist? Twenty-five out of twenty-five would indicate so. Could they all be Rembrandts or Renoirs or Van Goghs? Probably not. We do have our limitations. The point is we do not know our limitations. Perhaps one or two have more talent than the masters. They just never tapped it. Apparently, the art teacher had the ability to remove interferences to these twenty-five people's ability to reach their potential painting. What are the interferences?

Lack of confidence, inability to concentrate, poor self esteem, no training, not knowing where to start? Who knows what abilities we have that are not being reached because we have limited ourselves by interferences?

I am reminded of the story of a pianist who performed at an afternoon tea for a group of wealthy society ladies. After his short concert, one well-dressed woman came up and fawning over him exclaimed, "Oh, I would give anything to play like that." To which he replied, "No, you would not!" She was taken back. He proceeded to tell her "if you truly wanted to play like this you would forsake everything else, practice eight to twelve hours a day, take lessons and sacrifice like I have. If you did, you would probably be able to play as well as me, perhaps even better."

That really is the issue in reaching your potential. Whatever potential you desire to reach in whatever areas of your life, almost without exception, it has got to begin by reaching your health potential. You need to be healthy to be a success at your endeavors. To be healthy you must first resolve to do what is necessary to be healthy. Then it really is a matter of removing interferences to that health. Removing or having the chiropractor remove the nerve interference must be a priority. Remove those things that interfere with getting the proper rest, eating well and exercising on a regular basis. Then the causes of negative mental attitudes must be removed. You must remove the incorrect attitudes and perceptions about health that interfere with becoming a healthy person. That is largely what this book is about. Better health is for everyone. The decision is up to each person. No one can do it for you. All you have to do is want it badly enough, and then go to it!

• • • • • • • • • • • • •

A Word From The Author...

14

HAS YOUR PERSPECTIVE CHANGED?

It is our desire that this book has enabled you to look at your body, your health, disease, and even your life in a new way. If we can understand how much ability our body has in enabling us to be healthy, to stay healthy and even to heal ourselves when a level of health has been decreased, we have a tremendous basis for being healthy.

If you can begin to look at health as something you can gain, lose, improve, increase and decrease and that addressing health is far more important than addressing disease, your entire focus will change. Your life will not be reactive, trying to respond to the symptoms, the disease, or the outside forces that you are subjected to after they come. Instead, your life will be pro-active, doing those things necessary to maintain a high level of health and then living your life confident that everything is being done that can be done. One of the great things about an ADIO approach to life is that once you have done the things necessary to live your life as you should, then you can relax and rest in the confidence that your life is in good hands. When it comes to the aspect of life called health for example, once you have taken all the measures that you can take to be healthy, that is turning on the faucets, keeping the funnel open and patching up the holes that can be patched, you can relax, knowing that a principle, or power greater than anything the human mind has devised is in control of your health. You can be confident that the innate intelligence of your body is expressing itself as perfectly as possible in keeping yourself healthy.

Enhancing your life experience is primarily a life without fear. When your confidence is in the wisdom of your body you are not worrying about disease. When you are following the laws of health you do not have to fear the consequences of breaking those rules any more than you have to fear a state trooper with radar when you know you are not breaking the speed limit laws. Too many will never enhance their life experience because of living in fear. Fear of heart disease, fear of cancer, of the flu, of germs, of whatever is the latest disease that the medical profession has discovered. On top of that is the fear of the drugs and procedures to treat the disease that people fear. Understanding and living an ADIO world and life viewpoint frees one from a life of fear.

•   •   •   •   •   •   •   •   •   •   •   •

But the most important concept to understand is that it is your life and you must take the responsibility to enhance it. You will never have true health until you take control. A health care practitioner may give you information with which you can make better, more intelligent decisions but you must ultimately make them. A chiropractor may correct your subluxations but you must take the responsibility to be regular with your care. Someone may give you suggestions concerning exercise, but you must decide which ones are best for you and more importantly, you must do them. If nothing else comes out of this book, I hope you will take that responsibility and then work on those areas outlined in this book, so that you can truly ENHANCE YOUR LIFE EXPERIENCE.

●   ●   ●   ●   ●   ●   ●   ●   ●   ●   ●   ●   ●

About the Author

Dr. Strauss has been in the practice of restoring health and increasing individuals' life potential through chiropractic care for the past twenty-six years. He is the Editor of *The Pivot Review*, a philosophical publication. He lectures extensively throughout the United States and overseas on the subject of health and chiropractic. *Enhance Your Life Experience* is Dr. Strauss' seventh book. His other books include a novel, a history of straight chiropractic and texts used in chiropractic colleges. He also taught for sixteen years in a chiropractic college.